D1216459

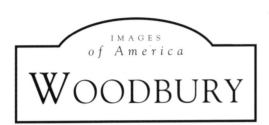

IMAGES
of America

WOODBURY

To Governor Al in appreciation of
your official visit to the
Woodbury Rotary Club on
January 23rd 2007.

Ed Molinari
President 2006-2007

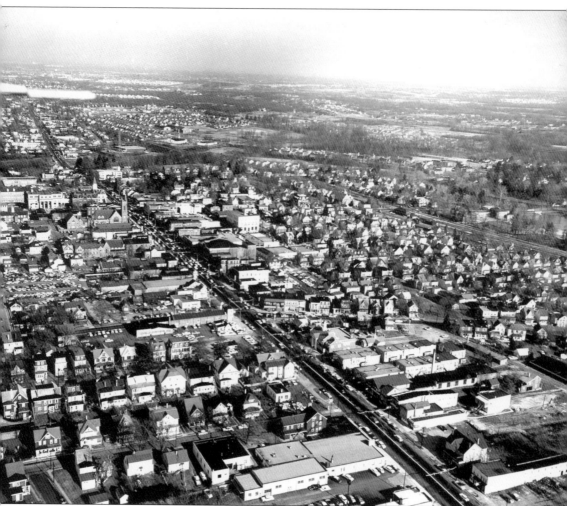

This aerial view of Woodbury taken around 1967 reveals the heart of the city. Becoming the seat of government for Gloucester County in 1787, the small hamlet of Woodbury had become a well-established community by that time. The old King's Road or King's Highway linked the village with both the communities of Burlington and Salem. Woodbury grew from the banks of the creek to what is now the business district along Broad Street. With the center of the community shifting from the stream, there was a demand for more roads, both private and public. This would bring the outside population to the focus of the community. Many of Woodbury's streets reveal the names of prominent figures who helped establish the community: Cooper, Hunter, Franklin, Newton, Green, Smallwood, and Tatum. By the 1950s, Broad Street had become a bustling economic hub attracting people from all ends of the county. Noticeable structures in the left background are the old Gloucester County Courthouse, Woodbury High School, Kemble Memorial United Methodist Church, the Presbyterian Church at Woodbury, and the *Gloucester County Times* building.

On the cover: Please see page 67. (Courtesy of the Gloucester County Historical Society.)

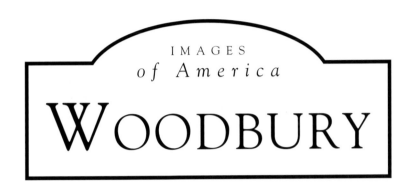

IMAGES
of America

WOODBURY

Robert W. Sands Jr. *and Barbara L. Turner (signatures)*

Oct 2006

Robert W. Sands Jr. and Barbara L. Turner
with the Gloucester County Historical Society

ARCADIA
PUBLISHING

Copyright © 2006 by Robert W. Sands Jr. and Barbara L. Turner
ISBN 0-7385-4645-3

Published by Arcadia Publishing
Charleston SC, Chicago IL, Portsmouth NH, San Francisco CA

Printed in the United States of America

Library of Congress Catalog Card Number: 2006928536

For all general information contact Arcadia Publishing at:
Telephone 843-853-2070
Fax 843-853-0044
E-mail sales@arcadiapublishing.com
For customer service and orders:
Toll-Free 1-888-313-2665

Visit us on the Internet at www.arcadiapublishing.com

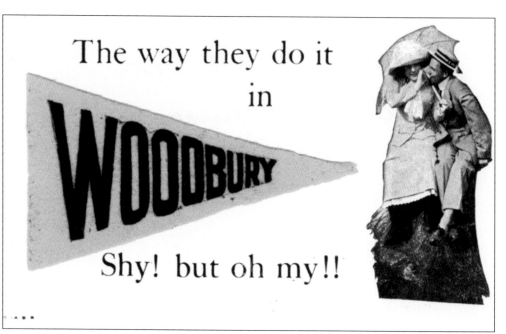

This vintage Woodbury postcard date is July 2, 1912.

CONTENTS

ACKNOWLEDGMENTS

Looking back over old photographs is always a pleasurable experience. The old saying "a picture is worth a thousand words" comes to mind. In preparing *Woodbury*, it has been a pleasure reminiscing about how this once small Quaker settlement has grown into a bustling community. We sincerely hope that this compilation of photographs will preserve the memories of bygone days.

Although the majority of the photographs are from the Gloucester County Historical Society's archives, several images are from private collections. We would like to thank those who provided photographs, some of which are being published for the first time, for this exciting and worthwhile undertaking. Special thanks are extended to John Adams, Robert Bartosz, Bethel African Methodist Episcopal Church, Mae Clemens, James Cook, the *Courier Post*, Charles Currier, Allen Eastlack, Walt Fish, Jill Leslie-Wiese, Lisa Holland-Foster, Adelaide Hetrick, Elaine Holt, Robert Littleton, Robert Long, Pamela Peterson-Wix, Donald Sanderson, William Wakemen, Judy Waxman-Monheit, and Mary Wilson.

A special thank-you is extended to the following for information and/or encouragement: Ruth Ann Cavanagh, Ralph Day, the Gloucester County Historical Society library staff, Peggy Lange, Dick Maier, William Mitchell, Eileen Shanahan, Bert Turner, Thomas Woodford, and especially Edith Hoelle for realizing that many years ago "a picture is worth a thousand words."

INTRODUCTION

In the year 1683, within the rural realms of Lancashire, England, fellow believers of Friends, also known as Quakers, rejected the king's order to worship under the doctrinal teachings of the Church of England. It was at this time that fellow Quaker William Penn gathered the brethren and traveled to the New World to establish a Quaker city, which he named Philadelphia, in Greek meaning "the city of brotherly love." Among those who came to America and established themselves as free believers were Henry Wood and his family. Sailing into the Delaware River, the Woods ventured into New Jersey and traveled into the Pesczackasing Creek, now known as Woodbury Creek. Along its bank they established a new settlement. By combining the Wood name with their parish home of Bury, the new hamlet was so christened.

When the old King's Highway was established in 1696, the road linked Woodbury with the communities of Burlington and Salem. This thoroughfare, along with light shipping along the Woodbury Creek, allowed the community to develop a strong commercial district. Soon consumers and merchants were attracted from all areas of southern New Jersey. As the town grew, it established itself as a borough in 1854 within Deptford Township and became an independent city in 1871. The economics of the city continued to thrive. By doing so, the rural farmland that once encircled the city made way for new housing developments. In the years following the Civil War, Woodbury began to be recognized for its lavish homes, constructed by Woodbury's prominent citizens. Among those was Woodbury's first millionaire and Civil War veteran Col. George G. Green. His enterprise of patent medicines became well known not only locally but also nationally.

Woodbury has hosted visits by four U.S. presidents: William Taft, Theodore Roosevelt, Woodrow Wilson, and Richard Nixon. It is a community that has produced a Civil War Confederate general, a United States senator, and devoted men and women of the armed forces from the training facilities of historic Camp Stockton to our heroes of the New Jersey National Guard. For well over three centuries, Woodbury has continued to attract people of many different nationalities, cultures, and beliefs. It is a city that has been able to balance its historic heritage along with modernization.

Woodbury preserves the images of this humble Quaker settlement that has grown into a leading community with over 10,000 residents. This book chronicles photographic images of the city from the 19th century to the late 1960s. Over the last century, the Gloucester County Historical Society has collected and preserved images of many of the county's communities. This book shares with you many of the photographs of Woodbury that are located in the society's archives as well as from private collections. We hope that these pages will bring back memories to those who remember old Woodbury and great insight for future generations.

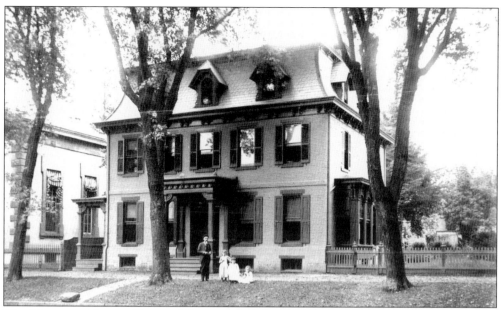

The Gloucester County Historical Society Museum building on North Broad Street was built in 1765. Over time, it was the home of three prominent Woodbury men: Rev. Andrew Hunter, Greenwich tea burner and teacher; Capt. James Lawrence, who coined the phrase "Don't Give up the Ship," and Judge John Jessup, seen here around 1900 on the left side. In 1924, the historical society purchased the home from the Jessups.

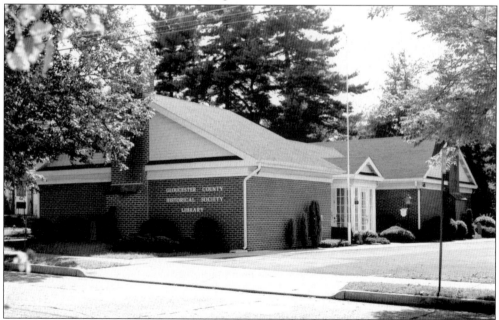

The Gloucester County Historical Society Library on Hunter Street was constructed in 1973; an addition was built in 1983. The original library was located in the museum in two rooms known as the Watkins-Stewart Library. The library contains over 5,000 vertical files, church and cemetery records, 3,000 microfilm reels, census records, and vital statistic indexes. For 38 years, the library was under the direction of Edith Hoelle, who retired in 2001.

One

BUSINESSES

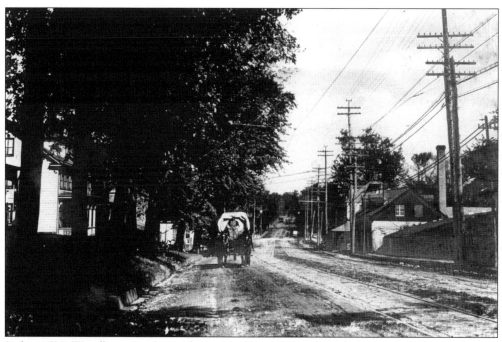

Before 1690, Woodbury Creek was the viable thoroughfare that transported goods in and out of the community. Between 1696 and 1698, after the center of the community's life shifted from the streams and waterways, the Great Road or King's Road through Woodbury was chartered. In later years, it was known as Main or Woodbury Street and finally was changed to Broad Street around 1854. It was about this time that the business district began to develop. Trolley service was established in 1894 and became an essential mode of travel. Horse-and-buggy travel, as seen in this *c.* 1905 picture, was still common. In the early 1900s, the Woodbury Creek was the dividing line between North and South Broad Streets. In 1927, the numbering system was changed, making Cooper and Delaware Streets the north/south dividing line. The homes on the left side of the picture are still standing today as well as the building on the right.

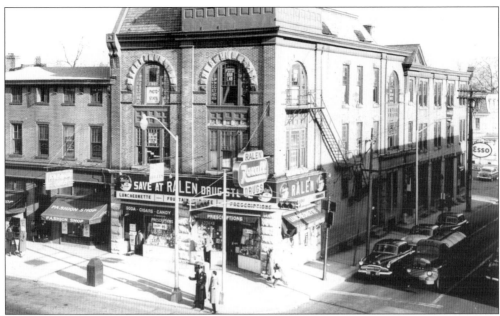

G. G. Green built this structure in 1887, and for over a century, the corner of Broad and Cooper Streets was known as "drugstore corner." Merritt's occupied this site for over 30 years. From 1910 to 1947, William Sutton Sr. owned the store until it became Ralen's with pharmacist Leonard Epstein. Lester Guggenheim's Fashion Shop operated next door from 1939 to 1980. Everett Fisler's Foto Bar Lab was located on the second floor.

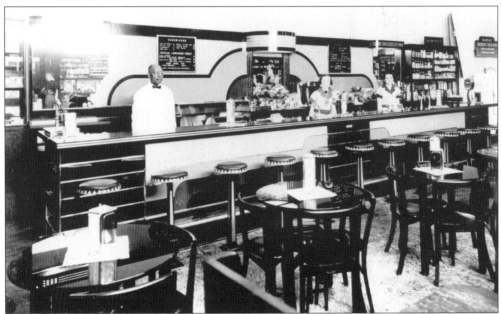

Clarence Fernandez, Elsie Wolfrom, and an unidentified woman flank the newly built soda fountain in 1936 in Sutton's, where one could purchase hand-dipped ice-cream cones or weighed pint containers. Lawyers and students gathered after a court date or at the day's end. Due to a fire in 1974, the structure was razed in 1982. It was the site of the former Lenape Center and is now Brown and Connery Law Office.

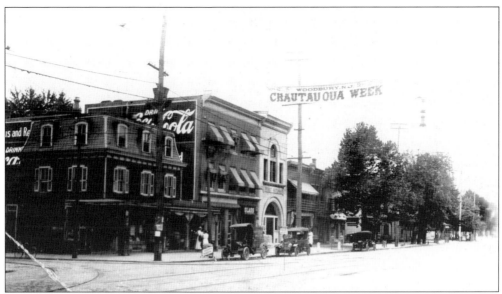

This southeast side of Broad Street at Cooper Street housed Engle's Barber Shop, Duffield's Oyster Salon, Schrenk's Bakery, and Hargrove's Paint and Hardware (Wakemen's Hardware) in 1915. The white building was the First National Bank, followed by Marshall's Drug Store, Coomb's Barber Shop, and Lay's Restaurant. Chautauqua Week, September 1915, meant a week of entertainment and education. Between 1913 and 1924, this organization arrived with tents, speakers, and professional entertainers.

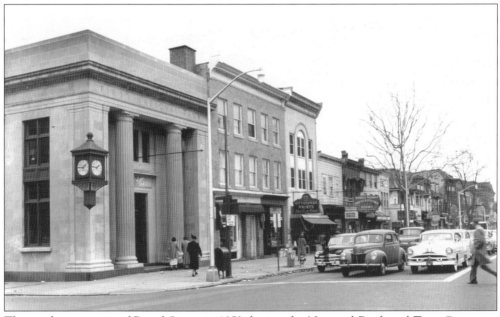

The southeast corner of Broad Street in 1953 depicts the National Bank and Trust Company; Schrenk's Bakery; William Wakemen's Hardware Store; Laurie Smedley Gifts; Marshall's Pharmacy, owned by Frank J. Maier; Ralph Kurtz's Homestead Restaurant; and Tip Top Men's Wear, owned by Jack Goldman. The National Bank, Schrenk's, and Wakemen's were demolished in 2000 to make way for the $16.5 million Gloucester County Family Court Building.

11

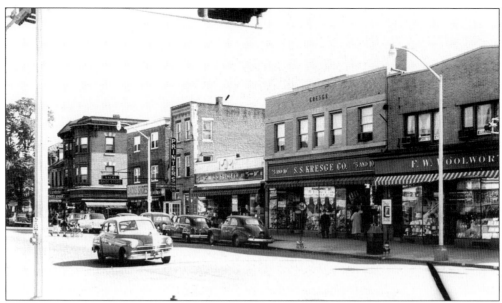

Stores between Curtis Avenue and Centre Street, around 1954, were Sacks Shoes, owned by Marvin Dickler; Williams Dress Shop, with William A. Becker as proprietor; and the Constitution Printing Company, operated by the Colbourn family. The S. S. Kresge Company and F. W. Woolworth opened in 1931 and 1937, respectively. In the far corner was London Men's Wear, owned by Israel Polsky. Woodbury residents enjoyed shopping the extended Friday and Saturday evening hours.

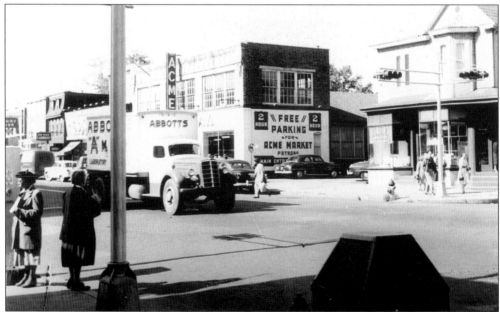

The intersection of South Broad and West Centre Streets in 1954 housed the Louis Schwartz Tailor and Rogers Jewelry. Acme Markets opened in 1939 in the former Budd Motor Company building, which later became Sta-Fit Health Spa in 1984. Sun Ray Drug Store, Jim Wing Laundry, Ruth's Coffee Shop, and the Dairy Bar followed. Mom-and-pop grocery stores became obsolete with the opening of the Acme Supermarket.

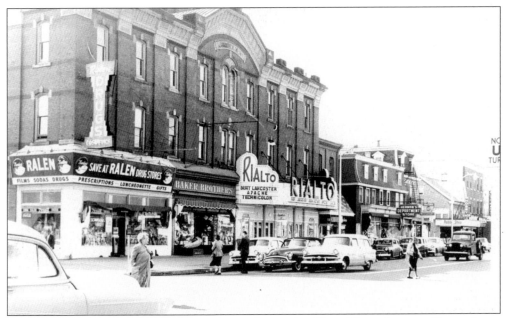

This 1954 picture of the Green Block on the southeast side of Broad Street between Centre Street and Aberdeen Place depicts Ralen's Drug Store and Baker Brothers. The Rialto Theatre, which closed in 1955; Howard Jewelry; Herman's Department Store, owned by Samuel S. Herman; and a restaurant rounded out the block. An insurance agency is now on the southeast corner that once housed Bob Kressley's and Jack Boggs' Hobby Shop.

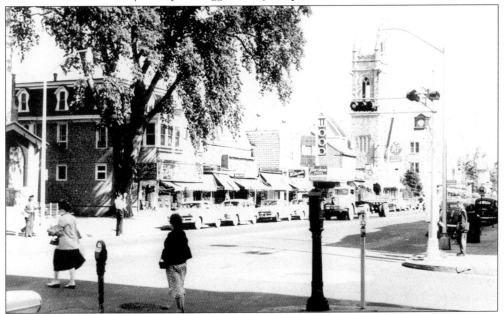

Looking north on South Broad at West Centre Streets in 1954 are Silver's Linen Shop; Robins' Book Shop; Benus Brothers Shoes, where children of all ages used the X-ray machine to determine if the shoes fit; H. C. Wilson Card and Gift Shop; Allen's Mens Shop; the modern air-conditioned Wood Theatre, which operated between 1939 and 1985; Romm's Hardware Store; A&P; Kemble Methodist Church; and South Jersey Furniture.

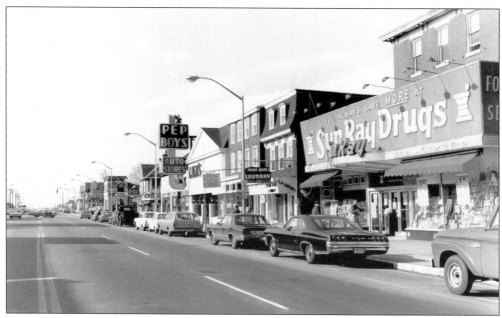

In 1966, Sun Ray Drugs was the place for prescriptions and sundries. Other businesses on the southwest side of Broad Street between West Centre Street and Barber Avenue included the Frank Mark Laundry, Louis Becker's Tailor Shop, Harry Lieb's Furniture Store (now Moss Rehab and Cettei and Connell Insurance Company), Pep Boys Auto Store, Snyder's Smoke Shop, Gulf service station, and Fritchie and Waddell Buick Dealer, now Barlow Buick.

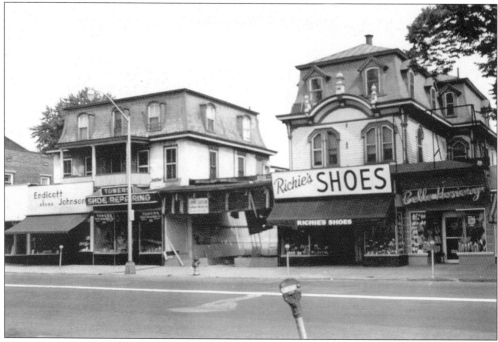

Shoe stores dominated the southeast block of Broad Street between Cooper Street and Curtis Avenue with Endicott Shoes; Tower's Shoe Repair, owned by Guy Basilli; Richie's Shoes, now Pilgrim Title; and the Belle Hosiery Shop.

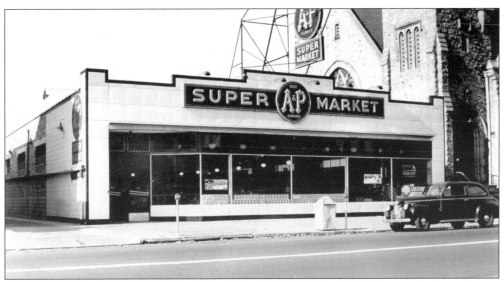

The Great Atlantic and Pacific Tea Company (A&P) was founded in 1859 as a mail-order business in New York City. The groundbreaking for this building on South Broad Street began in November 1939, and the business opened in 1940. A precursor to self-service supermarkets introduced in the 1930s, it featured private brands of Sunnyfield and Eight O'Clock coffee. Before 1955, the store moved to the Evergreen Shopping Center.

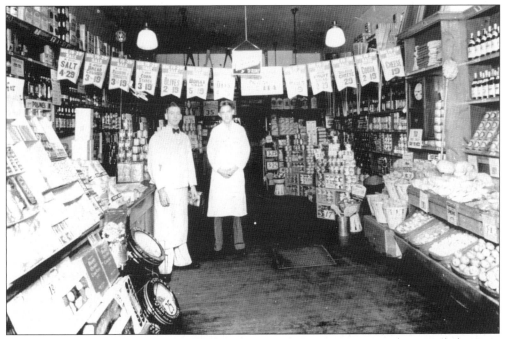

In 1918, American Stores Company was founded as a cooperative venture by several chains in Philadelphia. It became the largest retail food distributor in the world at that time. Pictured here in 1932 are Edwin Hill (left) and Francis Kennedy (right) in their store on North Broad Street. This store relocated to South Broad Street in 1939. In the late 1930s, Acme opened its first self-service supermarket in New Jersey.

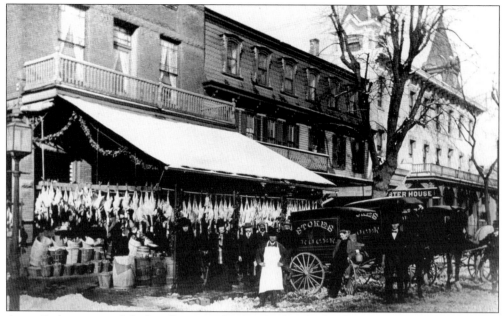

Anna Stokes operated Stokes Grocery after her husband's death in 1898. Known for "staple and fancy groceries," this store was located on Broad Street in the old South Jersey Furniture Store building, currently home of the Nut Shoppe. A 1909 advertisement in the Woodbury City Directory boasts, "Our wagons go everywhere." Stokes was known as the only source of green vegetables out of season and obviously "fresh chickens."

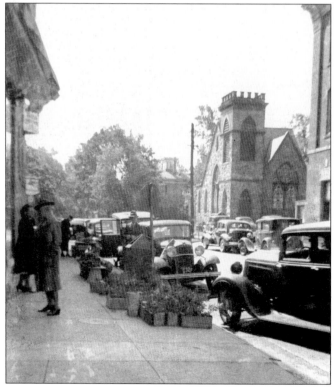

The farmer's market, pictured around the 1930s, opened in July 1918 on East Centre Street. It remained in operation for over two decades. Farmers from the county brought their fresh produce and displayed it curbside. This was the forerunner of today's Woodbury Farmer's Market, which is located along the railroad between Cooper Street and Curtis Avenue. The Central Baptist Church and the Green Building are seen on the right.

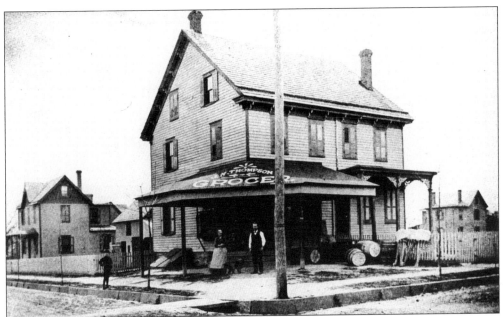

John W. Thompson Sr.'s grocery store on the southwest corner of Penn and Glover Streets was opened around 1870 and was in operation for three generations. Thompson's featured its own delivery service, which brought fresh poultry and produce to homeowners on a daily basis. The store closed in 1956 and later became the Colonial Electric Shop. Today the building is a private residence.

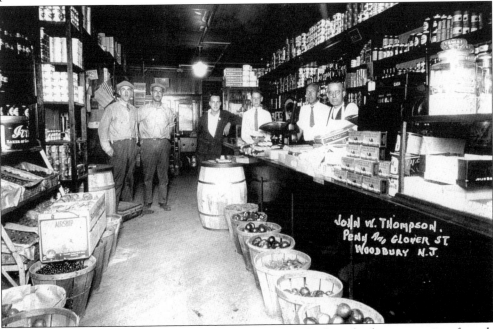

This c. 1940 interior view of Thompson's grocery store displays the large quantity of goods available. Pictured from left to right are Frank Hobbs, Albert Thompson, George Thompson, Bill Rambo, Courtland Thompson, and John Thompson. The lady of the house could call the store early in the day, place an order, and have it delivered by mid-afternoon.

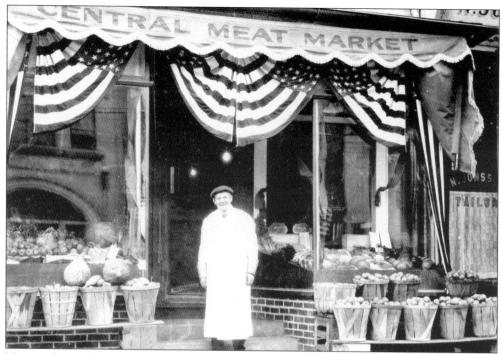

Meat markets and grocery stores were plentiful in Woodbury during the early 1900s. Pictured here is butcher Clement Anderson in front of the Central Meat Market on South Broad Street, just south of the Newton Hotel at Delaware and Broad Streets. It featured "Glen Rock Butter—The butter that makes friends—quality high, price low."

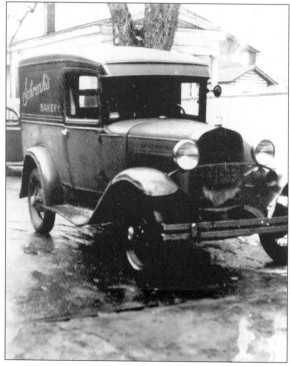

Schrenk's Bakery, owned by Charles Schrenk and located on South Broad Street next to the First National Bank, offered the best quality and prices on breads, pies, and cakes. During the early 1940s, one could buy a loaf of Freihofer bread for a mere 18¢. This 1930 delivery truck made it possible to offer "our delivery service at your door." This is now the home of Gloucester County's Family Court.

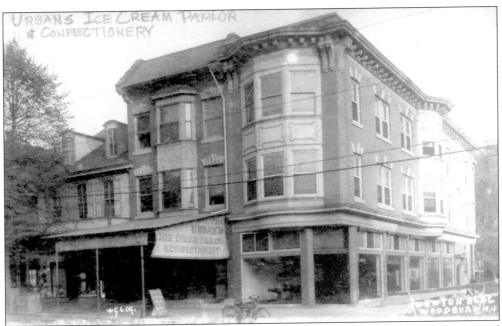

In 1920, the Bell Building at the northeast corner of South Broad Street and Curtis Avenue housed Charles Urban's Ice Cream Parlor and Confectionery. In a 1922 city directory advertisement, ice cream was "made of pure rich cream, sugar and the best flavoring of selected fruits and vanilla beans." This building now houses Pilgrim Title and Jackson Hewitt Tax Service.

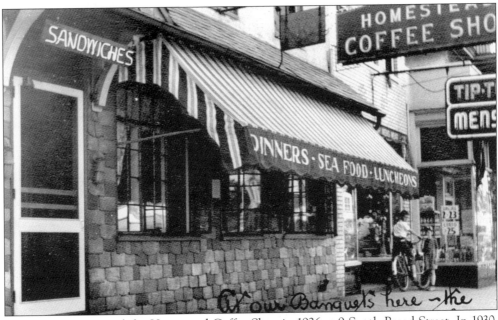

Elizabeth Kurtz opened the Homestead Coffee Shop in 1926 at 9 South Broad Street. In 1930, she moved to larger quarters across the street. After Elizabeth's death in 1931, husband Ralph assumed the management. On the 10th anniversary, the Georgian Room was opened, making way for various clubs to hold their lunch and dinner meetings. In 1940, Kurtz's daughter, Shirley Freas, became a partner. This restaurant was also known as Cafe Neena and Ristorante Garbini.

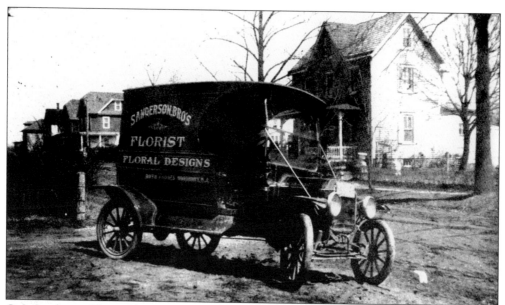

C. J. Sanderson Florist Shop on Morris Street has been in business for two generations. Chris Sanderson made deliveries with this 1911 Ford truck on many of the unpaved streets of Woodbury. This 1916 photograph is in front of Sanderson's greenhouse with Carl Neubert's house in the background. Chris's son, Donald, former mayor of Woodbury, took over the business in 1956 and continues to operate it today.

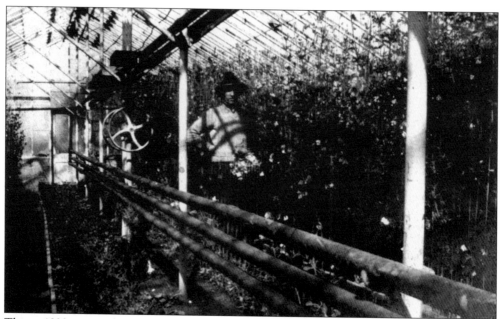

This c. 1920 picture depicts the rows of flowers grown in one of Sanderson's seven greenhouses, where they grew sweet peas, carnations, chrysanthemums, poinsettias, and the like. During World War I, they grew produce for the government to send to the troops overseas. Don Sanderson recalls cautiously climbing a ladder when he was a boy to replace greenhouse glass panes, which had been broken by tree limbs or vandalized by local children.

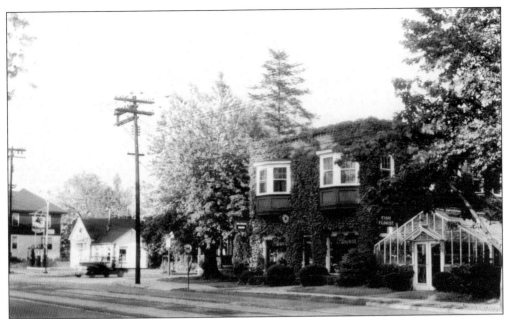

In 1921, Walter and Adaline Fish opened their florist business pictured here around 1935 on the southeast corner of Broad Street and Red Bank Avenue. Customers may remember seeing the large fishpond after entering the front door. In 1970, they sold the business to Bill Sennett. The building was razed in 1971, and Gino's became the first fast-food chain to occupy the site, giving way later to McDonald's.

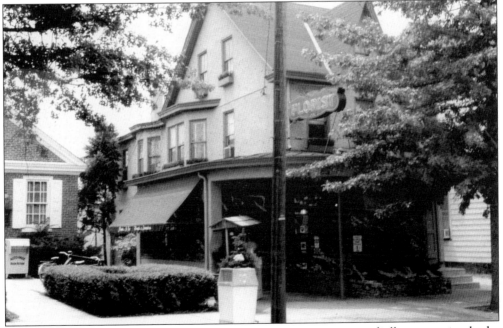

This 1971 picture of Sheets Florist at 45 Delaware Street, next to city hall, was previously the home of Ballinger's Florist, owned by Howard Ballinger. Woodbury students purchased many corsages for the Woodbury High School prom here. Dr. William Brewer started his practice in this house in 1896. Private offices occupy this building today.

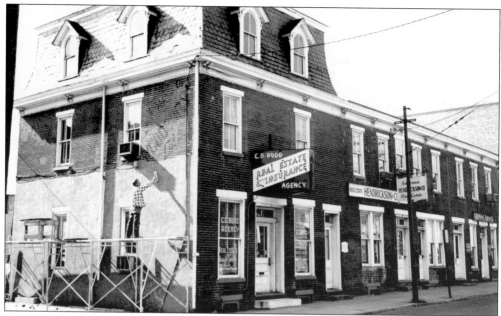

This *c.* 1950 picture of the southwest corner of Hendry's Court and Cooper Street was home to the C. G. Budd Real Estate Insurance Agency; Hendrickson Real Estate Agency, owned by Robert Hendrickson; and the Wilkins Agency, operated by Ada Wilkins. This complex once housed the A. S. Wilson Bicycle Shop and the *Woodbury Daily Times* on the second and third floors. The Gloucester County Family Court Building now occupies this site.

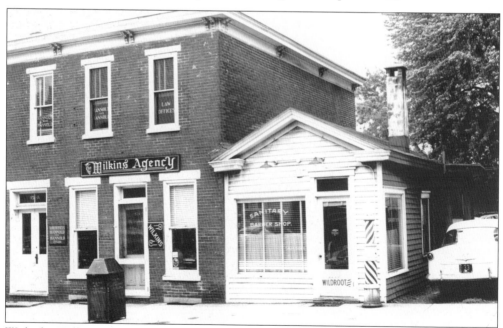

With the Wilkins Agency as his neighbor, Sam Sori operated a barbershop on Cooper Street behind the First National Bank. The business was relocated in 1954 to make way for the bank's drive-in facilities. Sori had operated his barbershop here for about 25 years before moving to Delaware Street, behind the Cotton Building. His son, Joe, later operated the barbershop.

This c. 1912 picture depicts the First National Bank and Marshall's drugstore on South Broad Street. The bank was located here from 1892 until 1923. It later moved to the corner of Cooper and Broad Streets. Marshall's, which now houses Edward's Hair Styling, was known in the 1950s for its after-school soda fountain crowd. Frank Maier Jr. operated the drugstore after his father's death in 1954.

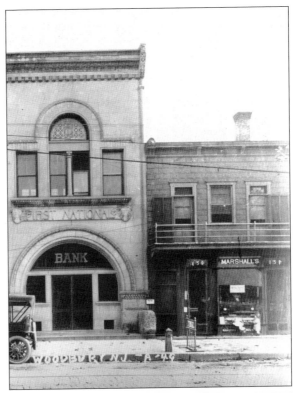

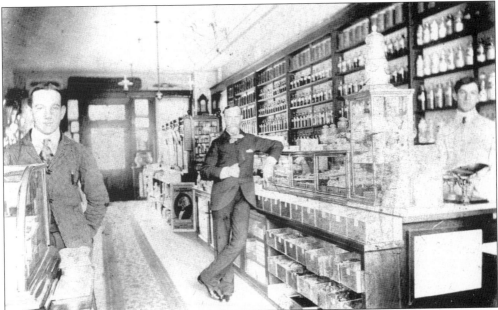

Marshall's Broad Street Pharmacy, established 1883, offered apothecaries of all types. After moving to a new location in 1895, it became the Eastman Agency for Woodbury. Frank Maier Sr., who began working for Alfred Marshall, founder of the drugstore, took over before Marshall's death in 1929. Pictured around 1928 from left to right are Frank J. Maier Jr., Alfred S. Marshall, and Frank J. Maier Sr.

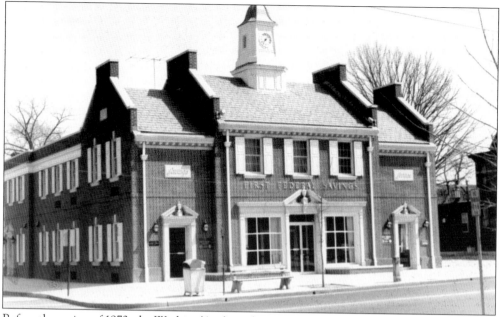

Before the spring of 1972, the Watkins/Andrews homestead on the corner of Newton and North Broad Streets had been torn down to make way for the First Federal Savings and Loan. This building has been home to several banks since then, including Hansen Savings and Bank of America. The parking lot property adjacent to the bank was once the home of John Cooper, as well as Lord Cornwallis's headquarters.

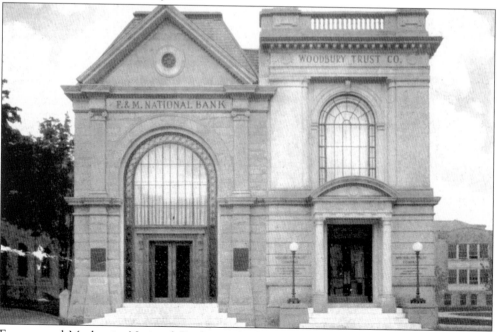

Farmers and Mechanics National Bank, on the left, was built in 1887 and operated on that site until 1959 when it was moved to South Broad Street. Woodbury Trust Company was built on the north side in 1915 and later merged with the First National Bank to become the First National Bank and Trust Company, with offices at Broad and Cooper Streets.

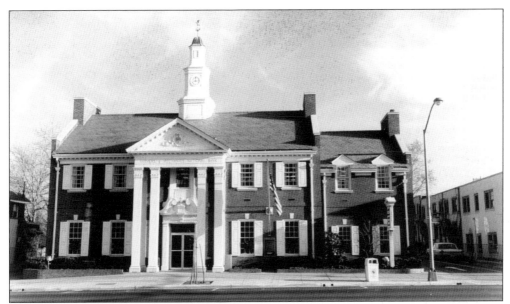

Farmers and Mechanics National Bank opened on November 30, 1959, in its new Colonial-design building at 220 South Broad Street. Groundbreaking ceremonies were held February 2, 1959, with the first spade of dirt being turned by James Henry, bank president. The general contractor was John Lawrence of Westville, electrical work was done by Roland McMahon and Sons, the rugs were by Sullivan Rug Company, and draperies were from Barry Decorators, all of Woodbury.

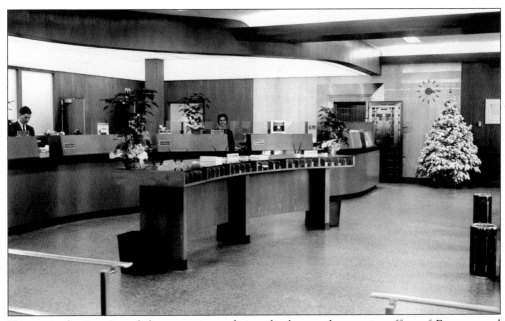

Shown is the interior of the new air-conditioned, ultra-modern main office of Farmers and Mechanics National Bank in December 1966. The hours were from 9:00 a.m. to 3:00 p.m. Monday through Thursday and 9:00 a.m. to 8:00 p.m. on Friday, with slightly longer drive-in hours. By 1969, the bank merged with First Peoples Bank of New Jersey. Wachovia Bank now proudly occupies this site.

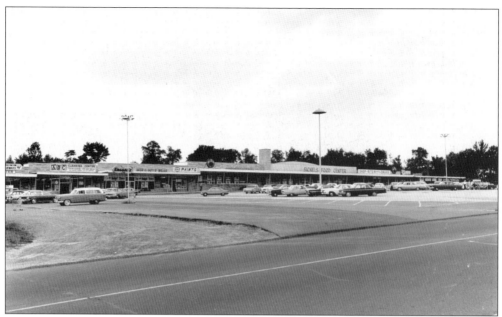

In 1965, Sickels Food Center on South Evergreen Avenue, built in 1954, consisted of a Raceway Center, ABC Cleaning Center, Ergood's Men and Boys Wear, MAB Paints, Shop-Rite Grocery and Drugs, and a beauty salon. The center was originally built by William J. Sickel and later employed his sons, Bill Jr. and Bob. It was the first shopping center in Woodbury that offered convenient shopping with ample off-street parking.

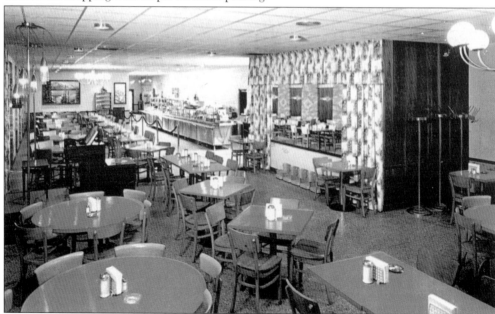

This *c.* 1960 picture of Ogle's Cafeteria depicts the red tables in what is now Weber's Cafeteria. Frank Ogle began his business around 1930 as a bakery on North Broad Street. Frank Weber, age 12, began working for Ogle by making doughnuts each morning before school. In 1973, Ogle sold the business to Weber, who operated it until 1988. Today Weber's son, Denny, and daughter, Sandy Moszkowicz, continue the business.

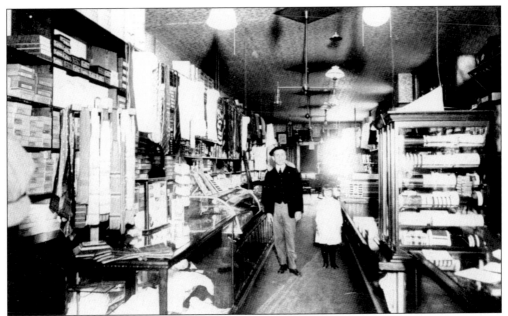

Shown around 1912 is Amos G. Wick's dry goods store, south of the Wood Theatre. Pictured are Amos and possibly his daughter, Kathryn. A 1909 advertisement listed dry cleaning, scouring, dyeing, and repairing, as well as ladies' work. Work was guaranteed with prompt service. This store was in operation from the early 1900s until before Wick's death in 1943. Around 1953, this site became Allen's Men Shop.

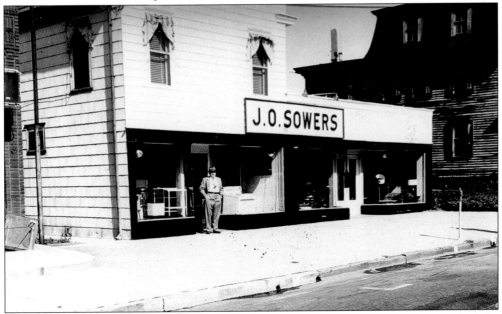

John "Ottie" Sowers stands in front of his furniture store at 343 South Broad Street, which he owned and operated from 1929 until his 1964 retirement. Sowers served as a city councilman and a county freeholder, and he was a member of the Woodbury Kiwanis Club. By 1976, this building housed the Goodwill Store. During the winter of 2005, the roof of the building collapsed, which led to the building's demise.

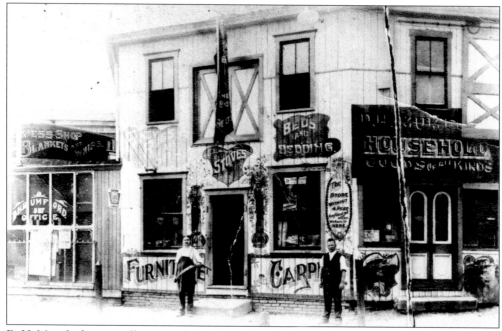

D. H. Mumford was an all-purpose business in 1915, advertising furniture, carpets, stoves, whips, bedding, household goods, and horse-riding items. The site at the intersection of Salem Avenue and Penn Street now houses Elite Auto Sales. Pictured from left to right are Charles Feltman, harness maker, and Robert Mumford, owner.

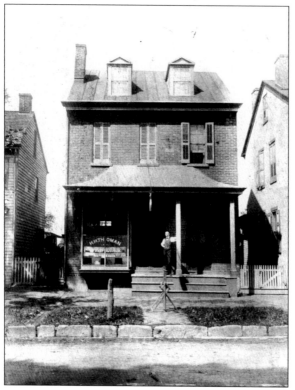

H. H. Thoman Jewelers, pictured around 1902, was located on South Broad Street and could supply anyone with the most reliable watches, clocks, jewelry, cut glass, and silverware. The store was owned first by Horace Thoman until his death in 1925, after which his son, Ralph, took over the business. In the 1950s, the building housed Romm's Hardware Store and is now Falciani's Law Office.

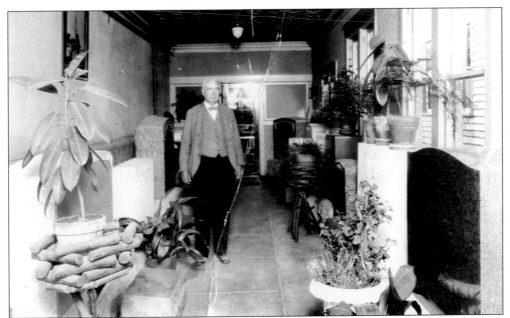

Pictured is William B. Snelbaker at 43 Cooper Street, who began his marble business in Woodstown in 1890. He was a leader in his chosen field and responsible for the monument at Red Bank Battlefield; the courthouse drinking fountain, which was moved to Hendrickson Park in later years; and memorials of significance to the activities of the United States in Europe, including monuments at Woodbury Heights and Paulsboro.

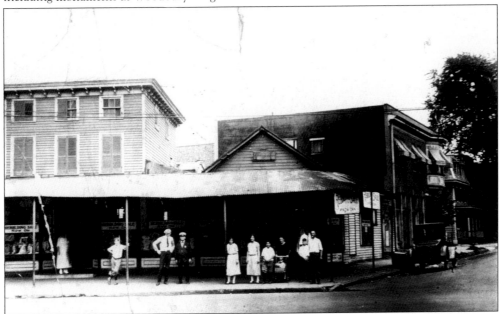

In 1902, Harry Polsky came to Woodbury from Philadelphia, leased this building at the northeast corner of South Broad Street and Barber Avenue, and opened a general clothing business. He purchased and expanded the store and then constructed three other small stores on Barber Avenue in 1906. The present-day building was constructed in 1925. Polsky's is still known today for work clothes, Boy and Girl Scout uniforms, and jeans.

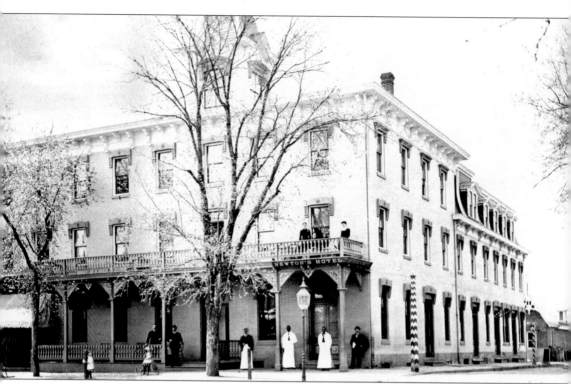

Newton's Hotel, shown here in 1888 and now known as Woodbury Crossing, proudly stood on the southwest corner of Broad and Delaware Streets. This structure, built in 1828, became a regular stop for stagecoaches traveling between southern New Jersey points and Philadelphia. About the time of the Civil War, it was owned by Adon Wills, who sold it in 1878 to Mahlon Newton, who in turn sold it to John Rachor in 1891. By 1900, it was fitted with hot/cold water, indoor plumbing, electricity, and steam heat. Rachor conveyed it to the Rufus Weaver family in 1919, shortly after Prohibition became effective. The Weavers operated the building as a hotel and dining room until Prohibition ended. In 1944, Charles Camp Cotton bought the building and converted it to mercantile stores, such as Lee's Men Shop, Robert Saloff Jewelry Store, Carmondy and Sons Opticians, and Newton Bar, with lawyers' offices on the upper floors. In 1976, the building was gutted by fire, and residents had to be evacuated. Restored in 1999, it now houses the Court House Café and Saloff's Jewelry Store.

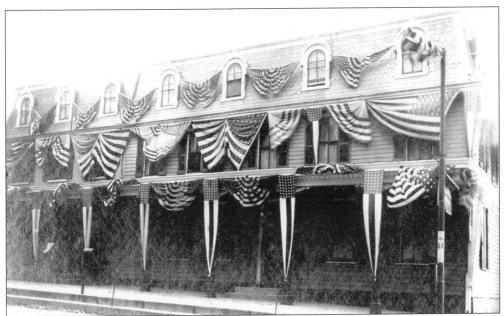

Hotel Paul, pictured around 1936 on North Broad Street, was built around 1715 and was a favorite stop on the Burlington-Salem stagecoach route. The first floor included a parlor, dining room, kitchen, and bar, while the bedrooms were located on the upper floors. In later years, it was known as Bulls Head Tavern and was owned by Ernest Stoerrle and Jim Cook, respectively. Today the inn operates as Charlie Brown's Restaurant.

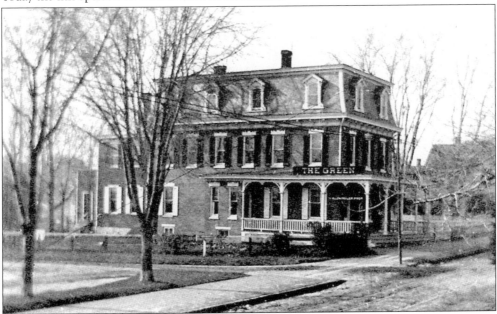

The Green Hotel, pictured here in 1900 at Cooper Street and Railroad Avenue, was built and owned by Lewis Green in 1881 to accommodate "dailies" arriving at the train station across the street. This building was later converted to one of Woodbury's first apartment houses. Roxby's News Agency, which later became Day's, was located here along with Lucille Goldey's grocery from the mid-1940s to the 1950s. The building is currently vacant.

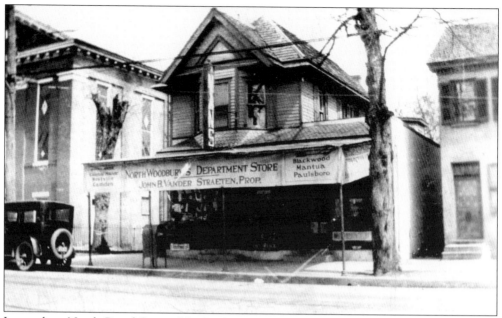

Located on North Broad Street, Vander Straeten's Department Store, pictured around 1930, operated from 1921 to 1936 when the Depression forced its closing. It carried a full line of men's, ladies', and children's furnishings. Adams Funeral Home was located here for several years before a Mr. Sweeten purchased it and moved the building several feet south around 1954. Today the property is occupied by the 1957 addition of the First Baptist Church.

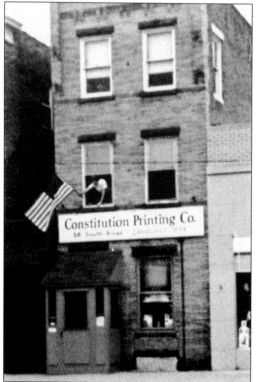

The Constitution Printing Company on South Broad Street, founded in 1834 by Augustus Barber, is the oldest existing business in Woodbury today. Two fathers and two sons, the Barbers and later the Albrights, managed this weekly newspaper company. The last issue rolled off the presses in April 1945. In 1946, Frank Colbourn became president of the company. In later years, Lew Robinson and Daniel J. Dewechter owned the company.

Woodbury Times paper carriers Bruce Mills (left) and Tommy Wilson (right) are ready to start on their route around 1970. Years ago, many young people made extra cash by delivering the *Woodbury Daily Times* to their customers throughout Gloucester County. In 1938, the *Evening News*, originally the *Gloucester County Democrat*, was sold to the *Woodbury Times*, which was owned by J. Frank Wilson, reducing Gloucester County dailies to one.

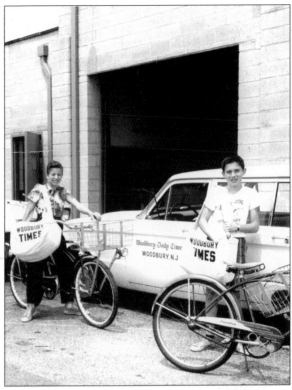

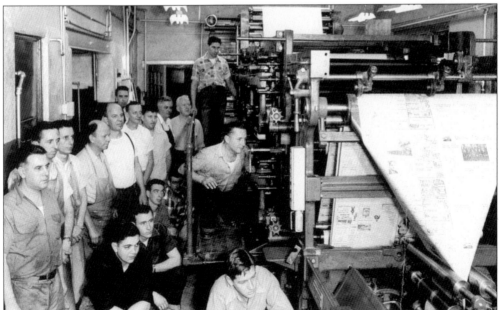

Woodbury Daily Times, which began publication in 1897, displays its new *c.* 1960 printing press. Standing from left to right are head pressman Michael Spirato, Joe Seddon, Thomas Fean, unidentified, Sam Alderman, Charles Warner, Jim Atkinson, two unidentified, Dutch Bayer, and Frank Wilson. Kneeling are Al Kirby, Bob Richman and unidentified, James Weber and in front, Jack Wilson. In February 1975, the paper became known as the *Gloucester County Times*.

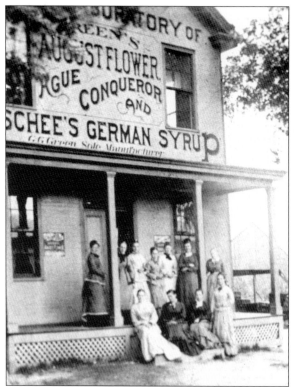

Civil War veteran Col. George G. Green started his medicine business around 1872 at Cooper and Green Streets when he purchased his father's small company. Pictured in 1873 are early laboratory workers of Green's August Flower and Boschee's German Syrup, which sold for 75¢ a bottle. If people suffered from ague, dyspepsia, rheumatism, or gout in the late 1800s, they could avail themselves of the colonel's miraculous Woodbury-produced patent medicines.

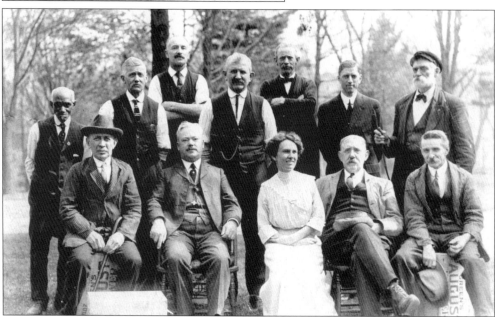

Employees of Green's laboratory on Green Street are pictured here in this c. 1900 photograph. Green's elixirs cured every ailment imaginable and were available worldwide. Pictured from left to right are (first row) John Estell, Col. Daniel Thackara Mathers, Alice Hoch, Charles Gebhard, and Howard Wilkins; (second row) John Dickerson (G. G. Green's confidential messenger), Charles Bell, Lewis Tucker, Fred Bayer, Eugene Horan, Isaac Carson, and Ben Brown.

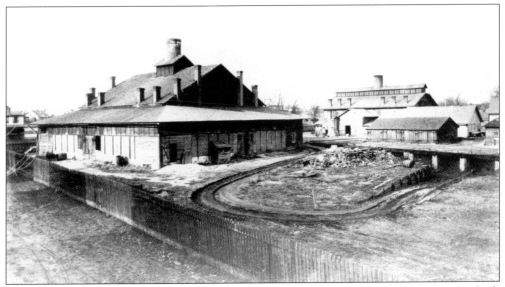

The Woodbury Glass Works in 1884 was one of several Green-operated enterprises, which changed Woodbury from a quiet Quaker village to a bustling manufacturing city. The demand for patent medicine was so great that Green decided it would be more efficient and profitable to make his own containers. The plant, comprising 11 acres, fronted German Street (East Barber Avenue) as far as Hester's Branch of the Woodbury Creek.

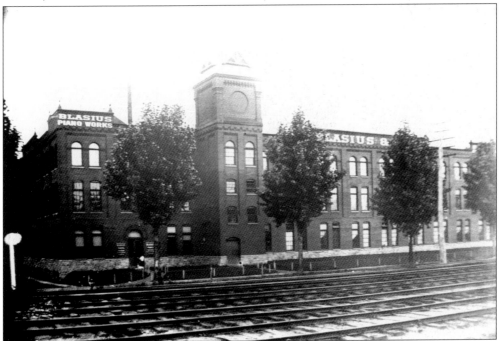

The Blasius Piano Company building, which in later years was the home of Belber Trunk and Bag Company, was destroyed by fire in 1970 in what was called the worst fire in Gloucester County history. Blasius, with offices in Philadelphia and a factory in Woodbury, occupied the site from 1888 to 1917. The building was sold in 1919 by its lessees, the Rice-Wuest Company, which were also manufacturers of pianos.

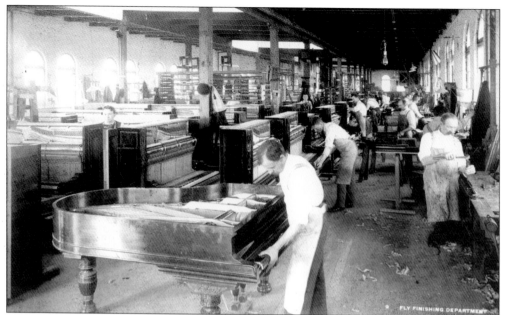

Unidentified assembly line workers of the Blasius Piano Company on Green Street are shown in this *c.* 1900 photograph. A 1914 advertisement stressed that great care should be taken in the selection of a player-piano, for not only must one get an extra good piano but a good player mechanism as well. In addition to Blasius Pianos, Albrecht and Regent Pianos were also available on their "easy-paying plan."

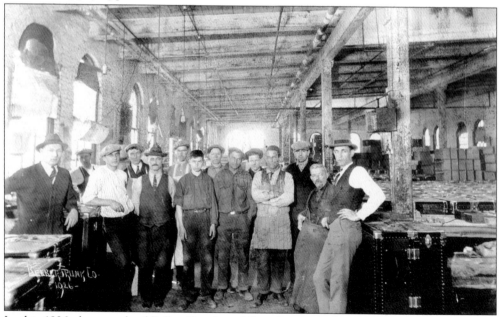

In this 1926 photograph of Belber Trunk and Bag Company, formerly Blasius Piano, workers paused before continuing the production of luggage, including trunks, pocketbooks, suitcases, and zipper bags. Belber relocated to Green Street from Philadelphia in 1919 and soon took its place as one of the leading industries of the county. Several officers of the company planned on relocating to Woodbury and its vicinity to make their homes.

Two

TRANSPORTATION

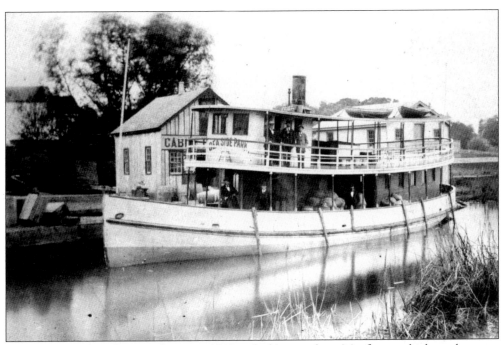

The river-creek boat business began in 1840 with the steamboat *Mayflower*, which ran between Bridgeport, Swedesboro, and Philadelphia. About this same time, there was the Woodbury packet named *Rebecca* that made two trips daily to Philadelphia with stops at the Crown Point Bridge. Water transportation played a vital part with farmers hauling their produce to nearby docks to await shipment to city markets. These docks were homemade affairs, but they served their purpose until new and better roads were built. The steamboat *Seaside Park*, belonging to Col. G. G. Green and pictured here in 1880, is docked at Green's Wharf near Wood Street. Steamships would stop here on their regular runs from Woodbury to Philadelphia.

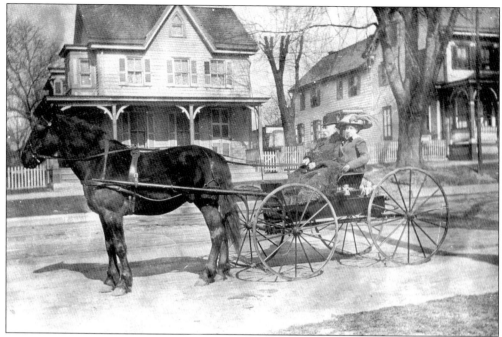

Horse-and-buggy travel was in its heyday in the late 1800s. Pictured here around 1900 is a couple "dressed to the nines" out for a Sunday ride. The picture was taken in front of the John Henderson home on South Broad Street, now the site of the *Gloucester County Times*.

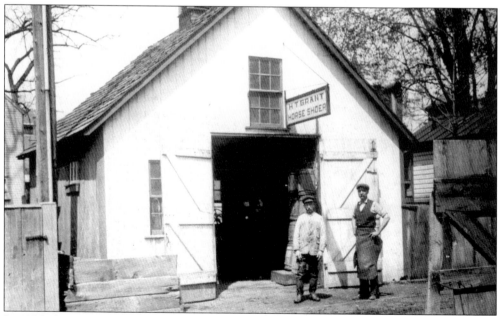

In 1895, the "H. T. Grant Horse Shoer" sign hung on Harry Grant's blacksmith shop, located on the west side of Hendry's Court near Curtis Avenue. Pictured from left to right are George Blake and Grant. Everyone had horses, and to protect their hooves, the horses had to be shoed. By August 1930, Woodbury was without a horse shoer, the first time since a shop of that nature was established here.

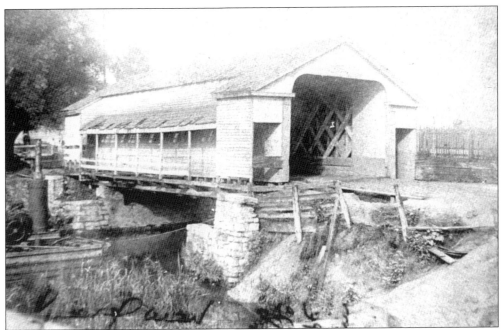

Before it was replaced in 1893 and raised nine feet to allow canal boats to pass underneath, this covered bridge spanned the Woodbury Creek on North Broad Street. When this photograph was taken around 1880, a toll gatherer collected one penny for each horse and buggy, while pedestrians walked across free.

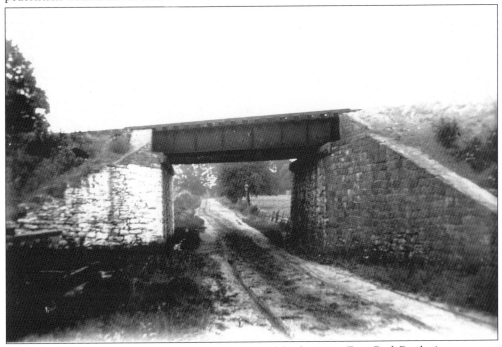

This c. 1886 picture is believed to be the railroad bridge over East Red Bank Avenue near Evergreen Avenue. Today this is one of the busiest thoroughfares in the city, leading to and from North Broad Street and Underwood Hospital.

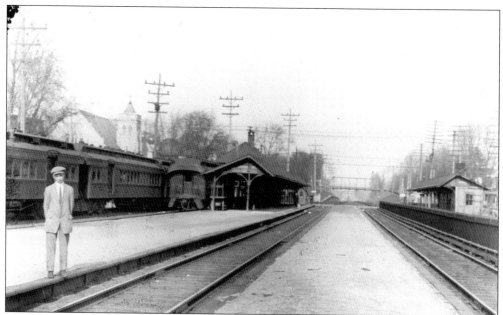

The Woodbury train station is largely identical to the original station from over 100 years ago when Colonel Green shipped his patent medicines around the world. This c. 1916 picture, looking northward, depicts two structures that were built around 1884 following criticism from the public about not having a suitable station for Woodbury to receive its passengers. The Hunter Street Bridge can be seen in the distance.

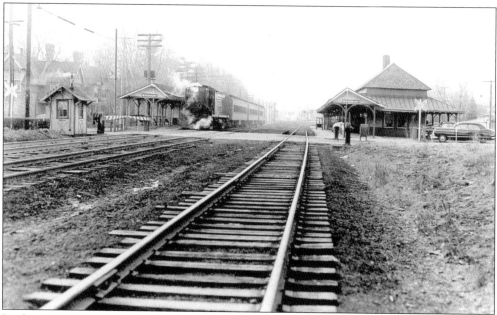

Looking south, this 1952 picture of the Woodbury Station shows the watchman's shanty on Cooper Street. The third rail, noticeable on the left, was installed in 1906, electrifying the line from Camden to Atlantic City. A third express track was later added as far as Woodbury to handle the hourly express trains. Salem and Penns Grove passenger service was halted in 1950. By 1971, all passenger service was discontinued.

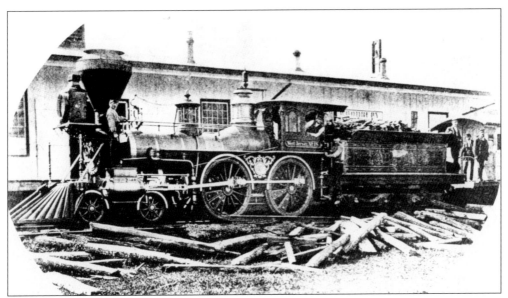

This West Jersey No. 18 locomotive waits around 1870 at the old Woodbury Station on its way to Swedesboro. An early timetable of the 1860s lists four daily roundtrips between Woodbury and Philadelphia. By 1917, the number of daily trains through Woodbury reached 139, and 56 of them made regular stops. Running time to Camden was about 25 minutes.

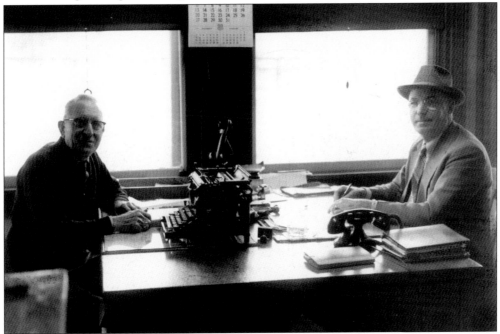

The Pennsylvania Railroad Seashore Line's Woodbury station on Cooper Street was a flurry of activity with passenger and mail trains arriving daily. Pictured in 1957, from left to right, are employees Harry Holzer, supervisor of track in Gloucester County, and Francis Evans, ticket, freight, and baggage agent. This station was renovated by Woodbury Old City Restoration Committee and opened in December 2000 as a restaurant. It is now the home of the Cooper Express Restaurant.

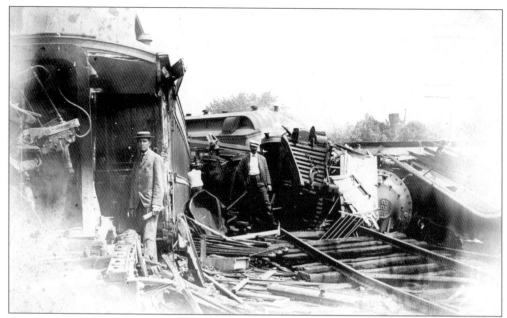

The Great Woodbury Train Wreck of 1904 occurred on the morning of August 5. The No. 5 *Cape May Express*, heading northbound, crashed through an open switch, derailing seven of the eight cars, as it approached the station. Eyewitnesses reported "the engine struck the switch, but was going at such high speed that she could not stick to the rails on the sharp bends, and rose in the air."

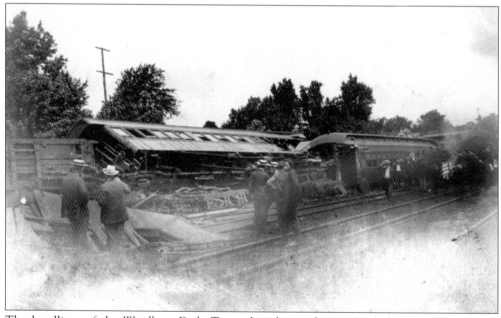

The headlines of the *Woodbury Daily Times* that day read, "A miracle how anyone escaped death in such a terrible catastrophe." Wreckage and debris were scattered everywhere. Seriously injured passengers were transported by train to Cooper Hospital, while others were cared for in local homes. The official statement by the Pennsylvania Railroad placed negligence on the switch operator and the engineer. It was believed that property loss exceeded $50,000.

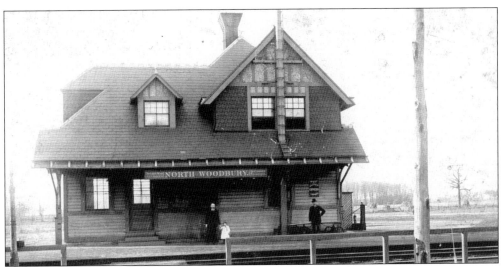

The North Woodbury Station, located directly west of Edith Avenue, was the getting off point for all residents at the north end of the city. This picture, taken around 1908, is believed to be station agent Lemuel Thurston and his daughter, Elvira. Before closing around 1929, Thurston was in charge of the station and lived with his family in the station's rear section and on the second floor.

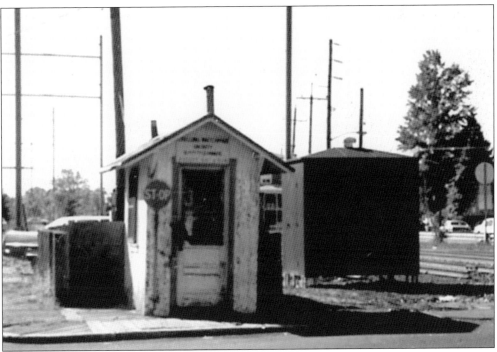

This railroad guard shack stood for over 50 years at the railroad crossing of Park Avenue and North Broad Street. The watchman alerted and halted motor traffic for approaching trains until 1985, when Conrail officials replaced him with automated gates and lights. The shack was preserved and moved to Hendrickson Park on the corner of South Evergreen Avenue and Cooper Street.

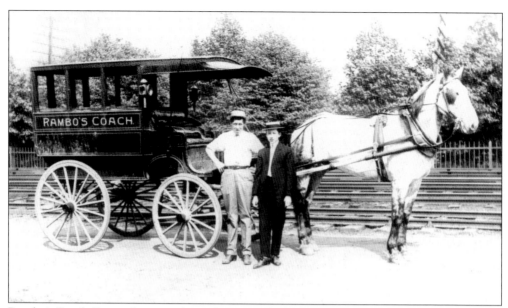

Rambo's Coach Service kept watch on the train schedule and taxied both local and out-of-town people to any part of Woodbury for a mere 10¢. This 1930 picture shows the driver waiting at the station for another customer. It was not uncommon for a funeral notice of a loved one to include the phrase "Coach will meet the 1:20 p.m. train."

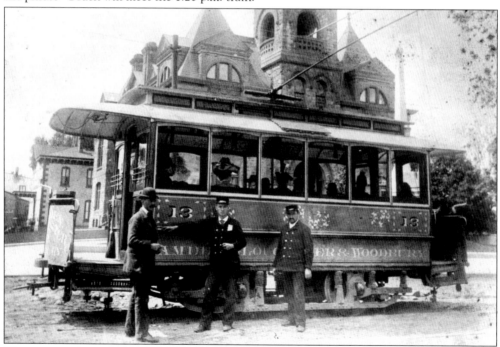

This picture shows Woodbury's first trolley two days after its arrival on May 12, 1894. The fare from Woodbury to Mantua or Almonesson was 5¢ on the Camden-Gloucester-Woodbury Railroad Line. In 1925, plans were made to eliminate the tracks on Broad Street south of Cooper since buses were in operation. The state highway department removed the abandoned tracks on North Broad Street from Cooper Street to Park Avenue in 1943.

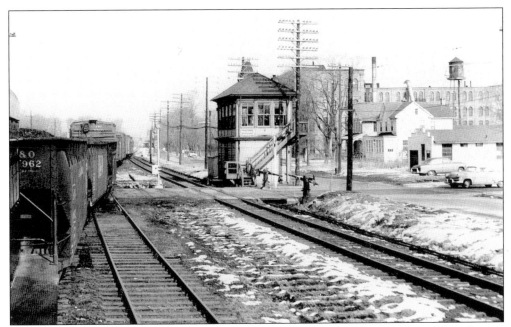

In 1906, a new interlocking signaling and switching plant was placed in "W Tower," later known as Red Oak Tower, located at the East Barber Avenue crossing. The tower was necessary due to the volume of train traffic arriving from Camden, Atlantic City, Pennsgrove, Salem, and Millville. This tower was demolished in 1956 when the building became obsolete following the installation of automatic signal equipment in the main Woodbury station.

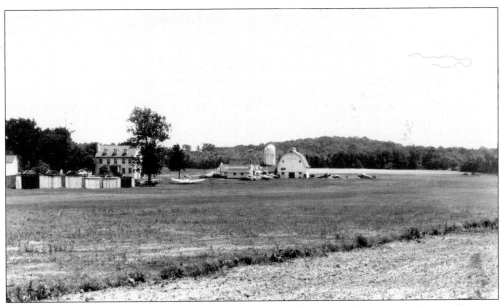

In 1948, Clem Budd's Woodbury Airport was located off Mantua Pike on the former Griscom property. By 1950, when Alfred Hill owned the farm, a large fire with flames seen as far away as the center of Woodbury destroyed the barn. In 1953, part of this area in West Deptford Township became Green Fields Village and Reeves Road replaced the former airstrip. Today this property belongs to Southwood Baptist Church.

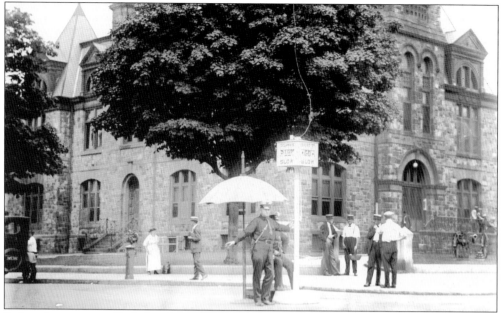

Before there were traffic lights there were traffic cops, as depicted in this c. 1920 picture of the courthouse corner at Delaware and Broad Streets. In 1936, work was completed on the erection of two automatic four-way traffic lights and a new traffic booth for a cost of $4,000. A traffic control person manned this heavily traveled intersection through the city during the daylight hours until 1982.

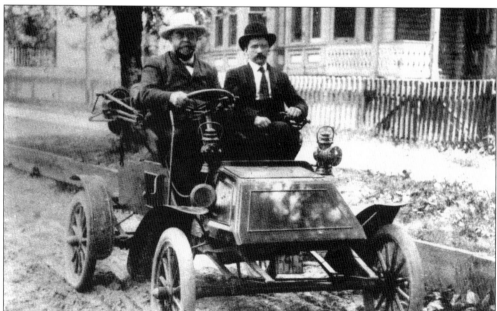

Dr. George Reading is seen around 1905 driving his first automobile, a horseless carriage, which was believed to be a French Duriet. The doctor, who had his practice on South Broad Street, always took Will Geitz along in the event that the newfangled contraption broke down. Geitz would then depart for home and retrieve the old reliable horse and buggy, return, and then continue visiting the sick with the doctor.

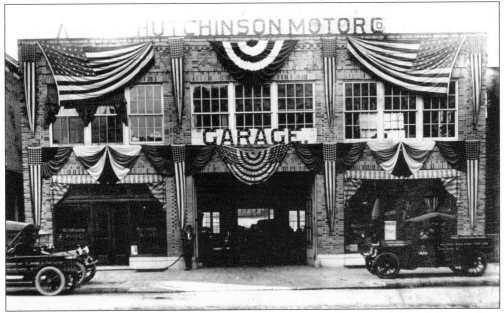

Hutchinson Motor Company, pictured around 1915, was located on South Broad Street where the Fitness Unlimited Health Club now stands. In 1911, after the company purchased this property, construction began, and a modern garage opened in the fall of 1912. The building was believed to be ample enough to accommodate the needs of the business, but the development of the automobile was so rapid that an addition was needed by 1916.

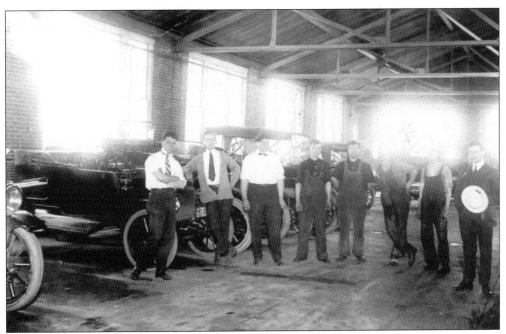

Hutchinson Motor Company employees are pictured here in the service area in 1912 in front of several automobiles due for repairs. Pictured from left to right are Tom Blensinger, Scott Atkinson, Tom Hutchinson, John Dietrick, Earl Wilburs, Joe Hill, Leon Laurence, and A. C. Eastlack.

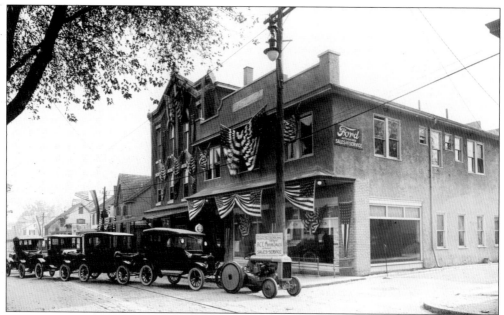

In 1910, James Eastlack and sons, Allen and Clayton, began their Ford business in Richwood. Upon signing an agreement with Ford in 1920, they expanded to 27 Cooper Street in Woodbury. After considering many names for the business, Wadsworth Cresse Sr. suggested Allen Clark Eastlack's initials, and from then on, they were known as ACE Motor Sales. Sullivan Rug later occupied this building until it was razed for a city parking garage.

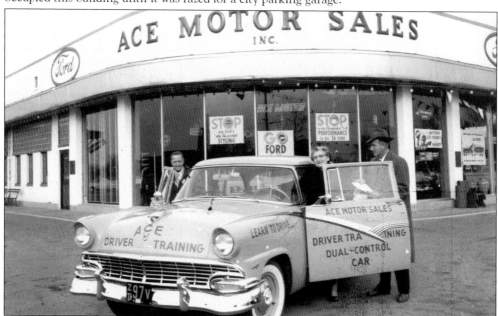

In February 1948, ACE Motor Sales, which had become one of the largest Ford dealerships in the Eastern United States, moved to its new location on the corner of Twells and Mantua Avenues. Construction on this building had to be halted due to World War II. Identified in this 1956 picture are Bill Mack (left) and Cy Eastlack (right) beside ACE's dual-control driver training car.

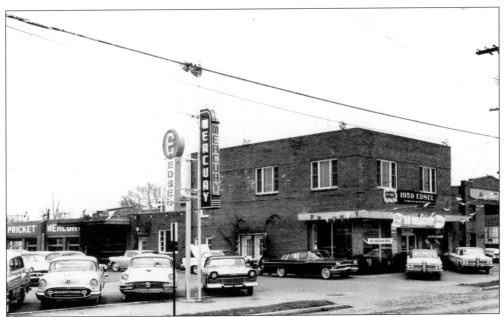

The Edsel made its grand debut at the C. D. Prickett Mercury Dealer on the corner of Mantua and Twells Avenues in 1958. Production began on the pilot model in Mahwah, New Jersey, in 1957 and ceased in 1959. In later years, this agency became Carter Lincoln Mercury Dealer. Many will remember being in the long line on Twells Avenue for the Woodbury Inspection Station, which is pictured on the right.

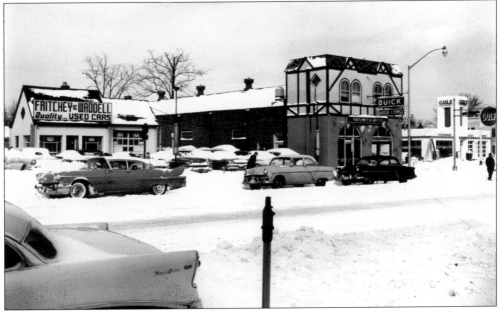

In 1923, Joe Fritchey and Rube Waddell moved their thriving automobile business to the corner of West Barber Avenue and South Broad Street. The agency continued to grow as a Buick dealership until 1965 when Ray O'Neil purchased it. Harry Polsky originally constructed this building as a movie theater in 1913 at a cost of $5,841. This automobile agency still prospers today under the Barlow name.

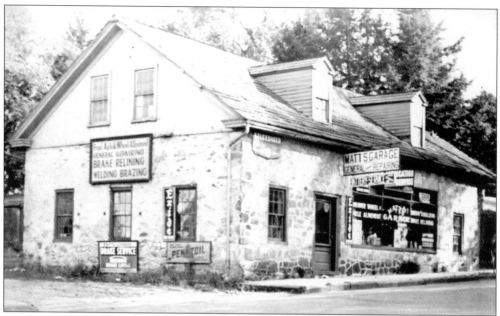

Matt's Garage, seen here around 1940, sat adjacent to the Friends Meeting House on North Broad Street. It is believed that this building, constructed around 1825, was built over the Hopper Graveyard. Matt's Garage later moved to North Evergreen Avenue. Other businesses have occupied the building, including Packers' Blacksmith Shop, Steve's Signs, and the Gloucester County Office of Weights and Measures. The county sold the property in 2006.

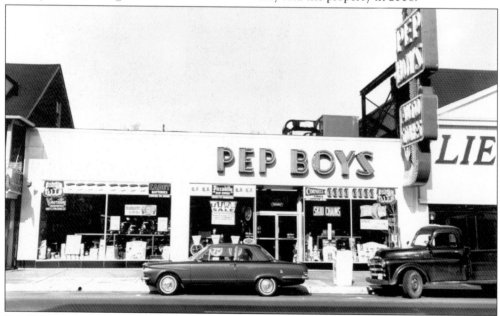

Pep Boys opened their store in Woodbury in 1938 on the east side of Broad Street. By 1966, Manny, Moe, and Jack had relocated across the street to their present location at 137 South Broad Street. It carried a full line of automobile and bicycle tires, as well as a complete line of automobile accessories. Snyder's Shoe Shop, later Rennies Appliance, is on the left, and Lieb's Furniture on the right.

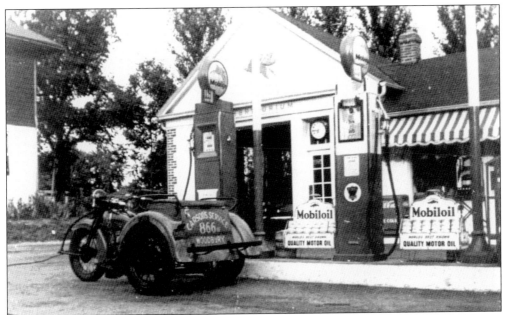

This 1940 picture of Carson's Service Station, located on the northeast corner of Broad Street and East Red Bank Avenue opposite Underwood Hospital, was owned by Alex Carson. "Your friendly dealer" advertised Mobil tires and batteries, accessories, and "certified Mobilubrication." After acquiring additional property to the north, the station, now known as John's Mobil, is one of the busiest in Gloucester County.

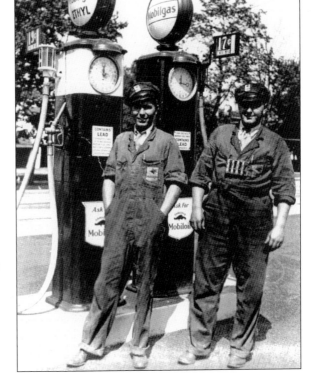

Pictured in 1936 from left to right are Alex Carson and Lee Coble soon after opening their Mobil gas station at 500 North Broad Street where they sold leaded gas. The invention of a lead additive for gasoline was part of the technological adventure of the 20th century. The Clean Air Act Amendments of 1990 mandated the elimination of lead from all motor fuel in the United States by 1996.

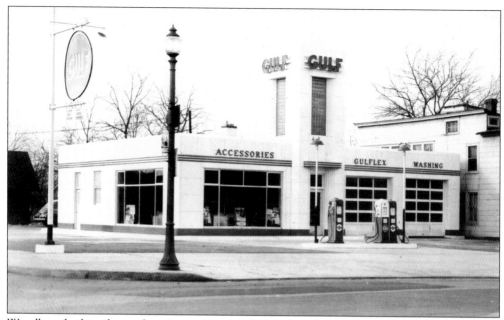

Woodbury had its share of service stations, as depicted in this 1948 picture of the Gulf station on the northwest corner of South Broad Street and Barber Avenue. After opening in 1948, it advertised "an expertly trained crew ready to give your car the best protective maintenance services possible."

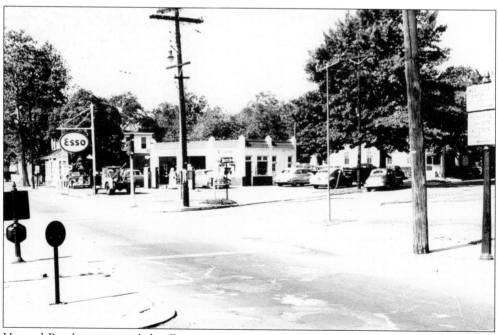

Howard Bundens operated this Esso service station at the corner of Salem Avenue and Penn Street in 1955. He advertised "repairs, towing, lubrications, tires, brake service and batteries." The Elite Used Car Agency now occupies this corner.

Three

COMMUNITY SERVICES

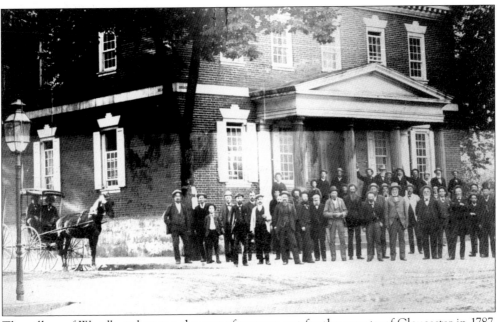

The village of Woodbury became the seat of government for the county of Gloucester in 1787. Prior to this, Gloucester County encompassed the communities of Camden and Atlantic Counties with the city of Gloucester as the seat of government. In 1786, the courthouse and jail in Gloucester City were destroyed by fire allegedly started by a jailed horse thief. It was decided by popular vote that Woodbury would become the new center of government. The courthouse, shown above, was constructed on the northwest corner of Lombardy Highway (Delaware Street) and Kings Highway (Broad Street). Freeholder's records indicated a pillory and whipping post were to be constructed in the public lot to the rear of where the Soldiers' Monument now stands. This method of punishment, which was considered inhuman and ineffective by modern standards, was done away with before 1836. In 1824, Camden's businessmen endeavored unsuccessfully to relocate the county seat from Woodbury to Camden. This led to the formation of Camden County in 1844.

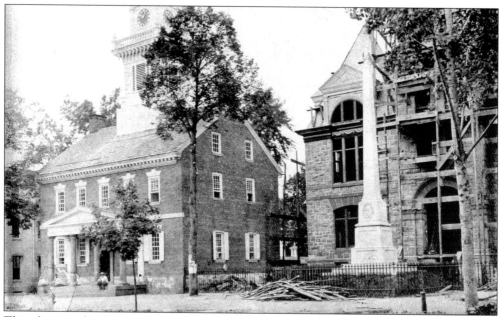

This photograph taken on September 11, 1886, shows the construction of the new courthouse (right) with the old one still intact. Signs of deterioration in the old bell tower deemed the building structurally unsound. Insufficient space in the courtroom was becoming apparent by 1881. In 1885, construction began on a much larger facility. Officials allowed the old structure to remain standing for its 100th anniversary before being demolished.

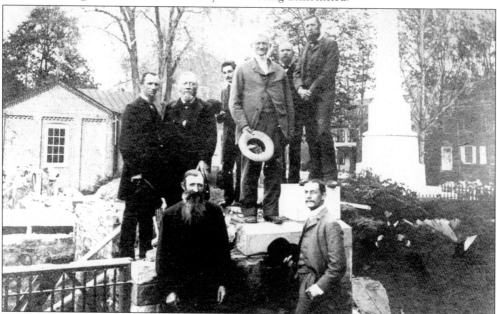

Officials pose for the laying of the cornerstone of the courthouse on October 28, 1885. The *Woodbury Constitution* reported, "The building committee . . . had not arranged for much of 'a time' at the laying of the cornerstone of Gloucester County's new Temple of Justice." The committee agreed a cornerstone should be placed and within it "a box containing papers and records of what would have historic value."

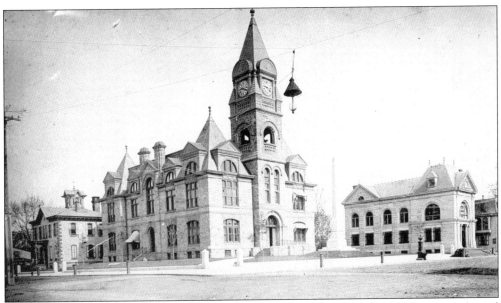

"Court house intersection" at South Broad and Delaware Streets, around 1900, shows the jail (left) and Farmers and Mechanics Bank (right), which became the Surrogates Office in 1960. According to the plans and specifications of Hazelhurst and Huckel Architects, William Steele, builder, agreed to construct this edifice for the sum of $64,900. A $990 clock purchased from the E. Howard Watch Company was installed in the 90-foot tower in 1886.

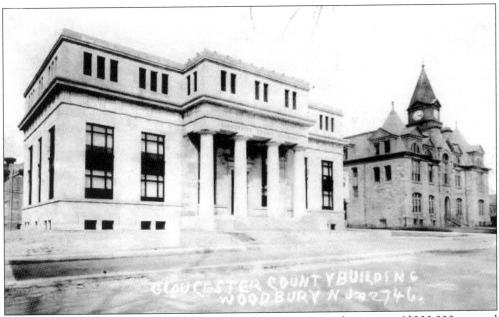

The Gloucester County Building on Delaware Street, constructed at a cost of $300,000, opened to the public in April 1926. This replaced the former jail, which was torn down in 1924. The building, which was connected to the main courthouse, contained office space, courtrooms, and a jail on the third floor. Students attending Woodbury High School next door recall prisoners calling down to them from the jail windows.

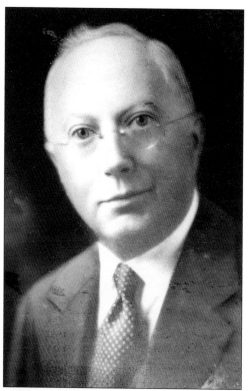

Dr. William Brewer had practiced medicine in Woodbury for 43 years until his death in 1940. Born and raised in Woodbury, Brewer began working at Merritt's Drug Store as a youth. He graduated from the Philadelphia College of Pharmacy in 1888 and received his medical degree from Jefferson Medical College in 1896. Brewer began his practice that year on Delaware Street and later founded Brewer Hospital in 1919.

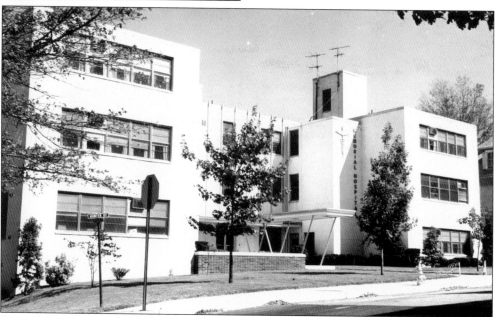

Brewer Hospital, on the northeast corner of North Broad and Hunter Streets, began in the old Matlock homestead. It was a 16-bed private obstetric and surgical hospital until Dr. William Brewer's death. At that time, the hospital, renamed Memorial Hospital, became a nonprofit corporation. On November 22, 1966, Memorial merged with Underwood Hospital. In 1970, the Memorial Pavilion closed, and a year later the county freeholders purchased the property.

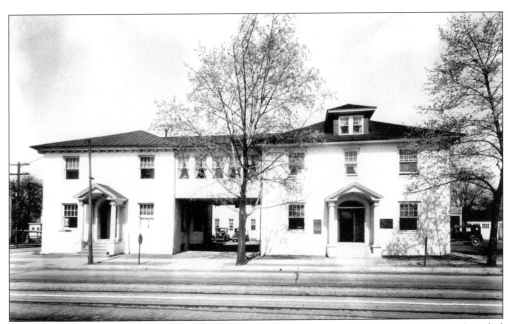

Underwood Hospital, pictured around 1920 at Broad Street and Red Bank Avenue, was founded in 1915 by Dr. J. Harris Underwood. Underwood converted the Columbia Hotel into a medical facility with dental offices for his brother Dr. Amos Underwood, a laboratory, and four rooms for patients. Additions were made to the original building until its demise in 1967. Today Underwood Memorial Hospital is the county's largest employer, with 1,770 employees.

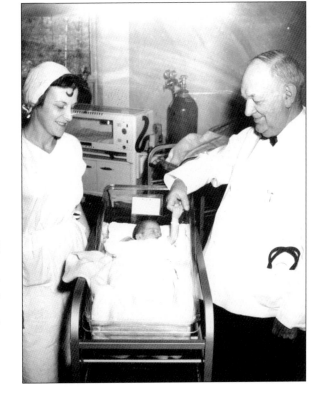

Nurse Doris Ives greets baby Fabrizzo—daughter of Samuel and Evelyn Fabrizzo of Gibbstown—and Dr. J. Harris Underwood, marking Baby Week at Underwood Hospital. This picture appeared in the May 3, 1955, edition of the *Woodbury Daily Times*, acknowledging Underwood's 11,326th delivery, on April 28. During the hospital's first two years of existence, Underwood delivered over 250 babies.

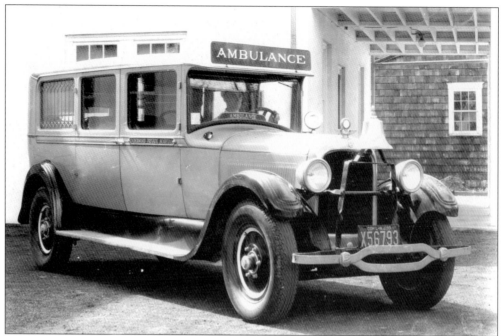

The first ambulance in the county was operated by Underwood Private Hospital in 1915 and was manned by volunteers of the fire company. An updated version of the original ambulance is pictured here in 1933.

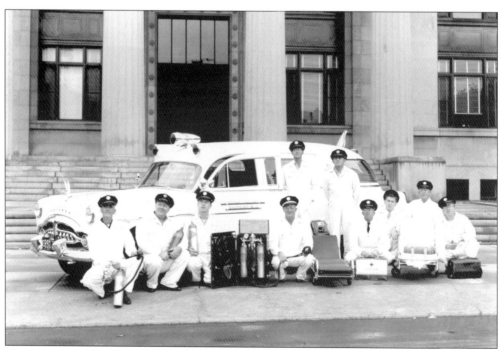

The Friendship Fire Company No. 1 crew poses with its 1951 Packard ambulance. Pictured from left to right are Harry Turner, Ray Cooper, Jim Bowe, Edward Strockbine, Pete Hughes, Jack Wilson, Charles Pettibone, Bill McCurdy, Gordon Bailey, and Doc Wilson.

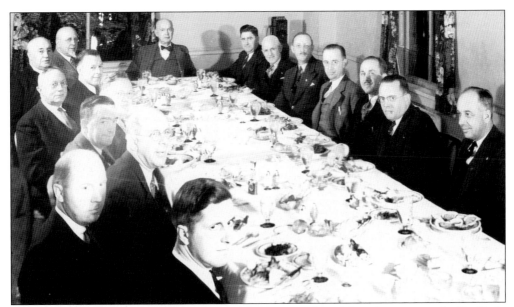

The Physician's Association of Woodbury and Vicinity gathered for a dinner given by Dr. O. A. Wood at the Walt Whitman Hotel in Camden on November 29, 1932. Pictured from left to right are the following doctors: Edwin Ristine, Baxter Livengood, Ralph Hollingshed, Fuller Sherman, William Brewer, unidentified, Harry Nelson, unidentified, Henry Diverty, Oram Wood, Russell Butler (chemist), William Crain, Elwood Downs, Donald Weems, Clarence Bowersox, and two unidentified doctors.

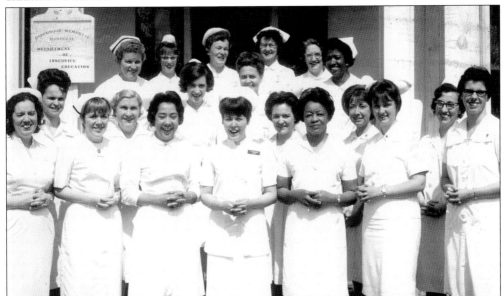

On May 5, 1967, nurses from Underwood Hospital's first ICU class gathered in front of the Department of Inservice Education. Pictured from left to right are (first row) Sarah Hughes, Marie Johnson, unidentified, Emma Klimanski, Helen Caliwan, unidentified, Fran Cunningham, Gladys Leary, Alice Black, Grace Braxton, Jan Rambo, Carol Power, Mary Bunker, and Virginia Cramer; (second row) Rose Murphy, Nancy Edwards, Gail Gartside, Alice Dubrink, Hannah Czgeladi, and Marjorie Pope.

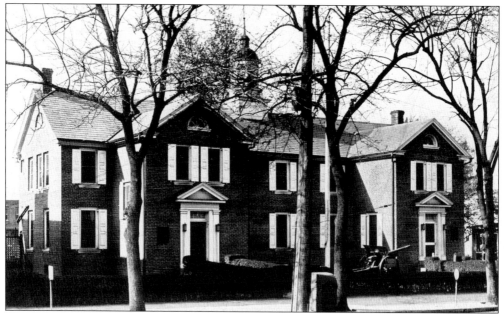

Pictured around 1925 is Woodbury City Hall on Delaware Street. The left portion was constructed in 1774 as the Friends' Free School, with a second floor added in 1820. The building was deeded to the city in 1893 with the stipulation that it be used as a library. A mirror image was constructed in 1923 for the mayor and city clerk's office, tax collector, council chamber, and Deptford Institute Library.

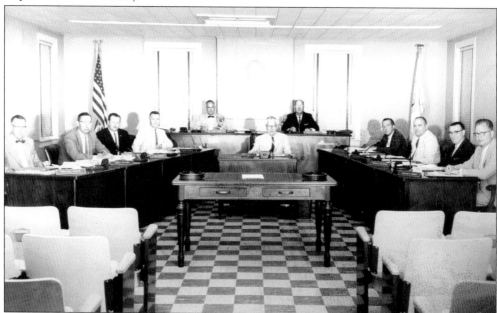

Members of city council gather in council chambers located on the second floor of city hall in 1960. Pictured from left to right are William Suback, Jim Butzner, Earl Renner, Sam Carver, Alex Carson (clerk), Walter Wilkins (treasurer-tax collector), Robert Brumund (acting mayor), Carlton Wilgus, Kurt Hoelle, Michael McGuinness, and William Riskie. The population in Woodbury at this time was 10,931.

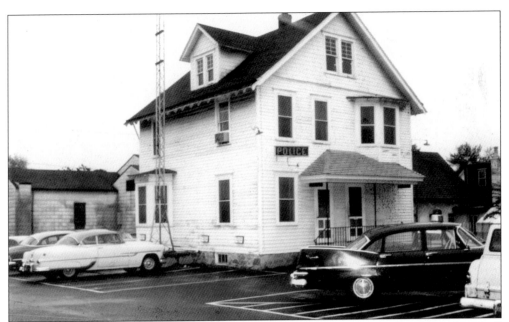

Woodbury's police department around 1950 was located in a renovated dwelling behind city hall between Morton and Russell Streets. Police protection began in the city in October 1876 when city council passed an ordinance establishing the department. By the early 1960s, the old police station was considered inadequate. One contributing factor was criticism from the New Jersey State Administrative Office of Courts, which claimed the facilities were too small and noisy.

Dedication of the
Police Administration
and
Municipal Court Building
Woodbury, New Jersey

July 4, 1962

By 1962, construction had begun on a new Colonial-style police station on the east side of North Broad Street, just south of Woodbury Creek. The new structure was furnished with the most modern technology and was considered one of the finest facilities in the country. The dedication and cornerstone-laying ceremonies were held on the Fourth of July of that year, with remarks from city leaders.

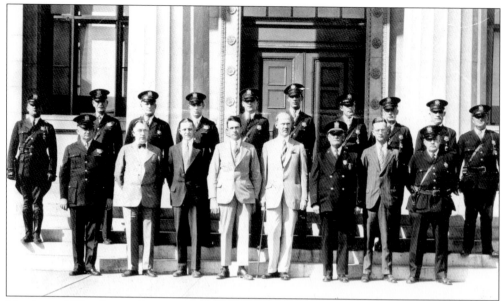

Members of Woodbury's finest gather on Delaware Street in 1930. Pictured from left to right are (first row) James Lynch, councilman James Morgan, Henry Doerrman (public safety committee), Ted Curtis, Mayor Ernest Rigg, Chief Burton Magee, William Menah (public safety committee), and William Porch; (second row) Nick Comishock, Barry Sheppard, Jack Keegan, Ralph Braithwood, Bob Lutz, Jacob Yearicks, Herman Peters, George Carey, Ed Hampton, and Emerson Goldy.

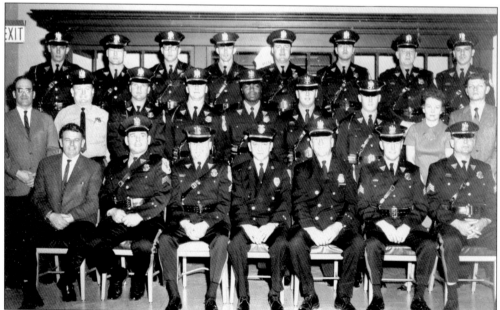

Pictured in this 1973 Woodbury Police Department photograph, from left to right, are (first row) Bob Malin, Donald Rea, Bob Littleton, Chief Dean Kimmel, Lt. George Schmidt, Bill Volk, and Harold Gilcrest; (second row) Ralph Quindone, Buster Jacobs, Jeff Wright, Joe Szolack, Luke Ivey, Herb Bakely, John Nelson, Ann Grey, and Dick Henry; (third row) Whit Reddin, Davis Harrell, Don Trout, Earl Muhlbaier, Vic Simonia, Joe Anthony, Harold Bock, and Irv Kimmel.

In March 1960, Gray and Fear lowered a new Colonial-style cupola into place atop the Friendship Fire Company's bell tower. The Woodbury Fire Company was established in 1799 and was succeeded in name and ownership by Friendship in 1830. Ground was broken in September 1898 for the present firehouse at a cost of $6,125. It was designed to house equipment and horses and has been renovated several times since.

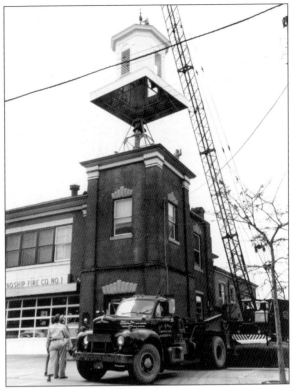

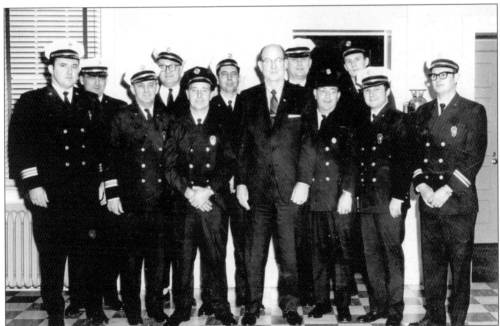

In 1970, fire officers from Friendship and Goodwill posed for this picture. From left to right are Chief Ray Sweeney, Capt. Dave Laverty, Deputy Chief Frank Strockbine, Capt. Bob Mount, Lt. Chess Walcott, Capt. Tom Fountain, Mayor Bob Brummund, Capt. Don Davis, Lt. Art Morely, Lt. Jim Hesser, Battalion Chief Dick Wagner, and Battalion Chief Bill Wakemen.

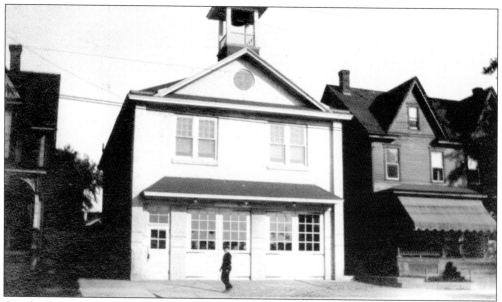

Goodwill Fire Company No. 2 was chartered on April 22, 1889, after several North Woodbury citizens became concerned that only one fire company would be capable of covering the fast-growing community. The present structure, seen here around 1925, was built in 1922 after outgrowing its former facilities, located across the street. In 2006, city council voted to merge Goodwill and Friendship Fire Companies, thus closing Goodwill's facilities.

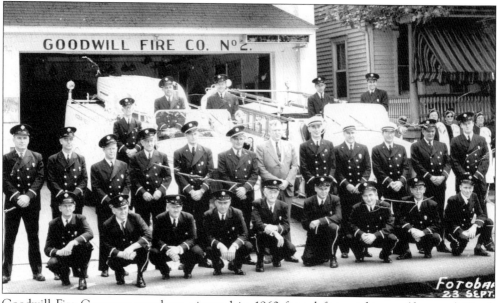

Goodwill Fire Company members, pictured in 1960 from left to right, are (first row) Frank Maier, Charles Bengel, Charles McFadden, Joe Gill, Calvin Black, Al Bock, Jim Wilgus, Bob Miley, and John Sparks; (second row) Kurt Hoelle, Earl Tapper, Les Harker, Bert Dopson, Leon Creivier, Vic Gray, David Brewer (medical advisor), Al Lutz (chief), Les Littley, Carlton Wilgus, Leon Youngcourt, and Walt Fish (president); (third row) Les Tweed, Joe Sarlo, Bert Lancaster, unidentified, and Jimmy Sacca.

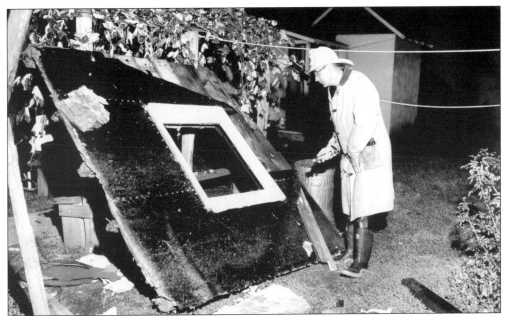

On the night of June 15, 1961, this Allen Lane home was blown apart by a leaking propane gas tank. The blast, ignited by a kerosene space heater, leveled the two-room dwelling occupied by Murray Sims. He was tossed 40 feet from the dwelling and rushed to Underwood Hospital. The explosion, which occurred about 11:15 p.m., rocked neighboring homes and shattered windows. Both city fire departments responded to the call.

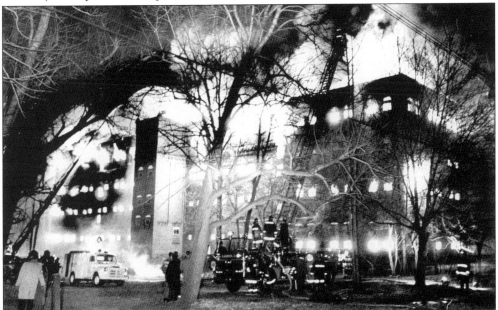

"Belber building razed in city's largest fire" read the headlines of the *Woodbury Times* on March 10, 1970. Over 400 firefighters from neighboring communities assisted in what was considered Woodbury's worst fire on record. The blaze, which was reported at 8:10 p.m., could be seen from the Walt Whitman Bridge some 11 miles away. Flying embers and falling bricks made conditions dangerous. The blaze took nearly 24 hours to fully extinguish.

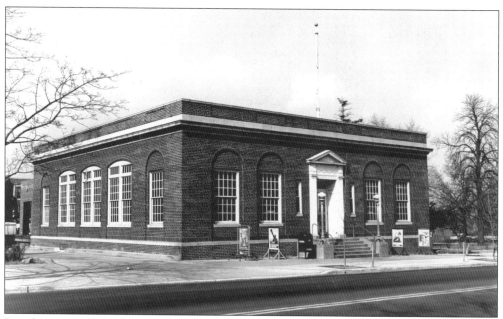

Postal service in Woodbury began when Congress established a postal department in 1792. The first post office was located on Cooper Street and later moved in 1892 to Merritt's Drug Store. To meet the growing demands of the community, a $50,000 brick facility was constructed in 1924 on Broad Street in front of Woodbury High School. The building was opened to the public on May 4, 1925.

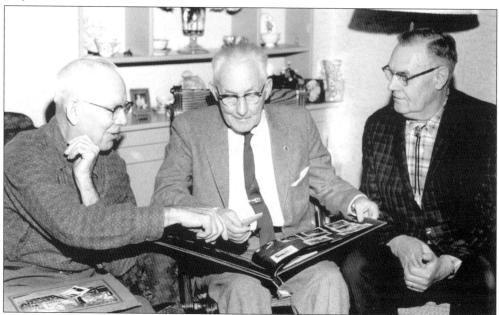

Free mail delivery in Woodbury began in 1902 with carriers receiving an annual salary of $600. In order to become a mail carrier, applicants had to be at least 5 feet 4 inches in height exclusive of boots or shoes and weigh at least 125 pounds. Former Woodbury carriers William Beck, John Craig, and John Grant reminisce in December 1964 about their years as Woodbury mail carriers.

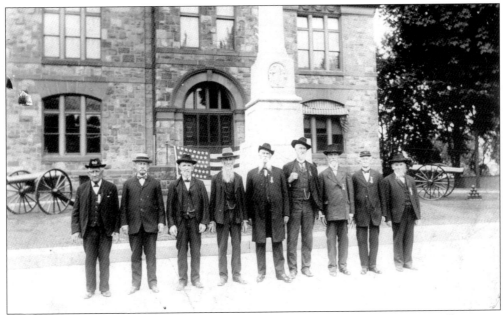

The last surviving Civil War veterans of the General Joshua Howell Post of Woodbury pose around 1920 in front of the courthouse. At a meeting of Civil War Veterans in July 1879, the Grand Army of the Republic (GAR) Post 31 was formed. From left to right are William Dopson, W. Harrison Livermore, Charles Smith, James Hutchinson, Joshua Dawson, W. Thackara Cozens, Joseph Morgan, Lewis Sparks, and James Davies.

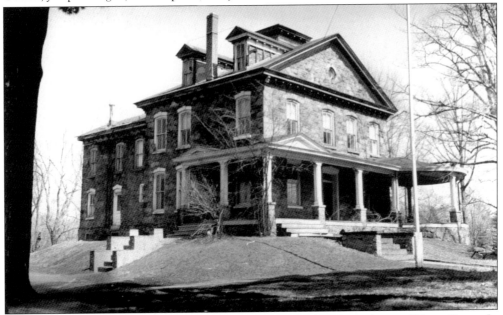

The American Legion Hall, pictured here in 1967, was the former residence of Harry Green. In 1948, this became the home of the William Stokes Bonsal Post No. 133 and where the Bonsal Blues Band originated. During the 1960s, the Woodbury Jaycees met here on a weekly basis. The post moved about 1975 to their new location on Washington Avenue, and the earlier building was demolished.

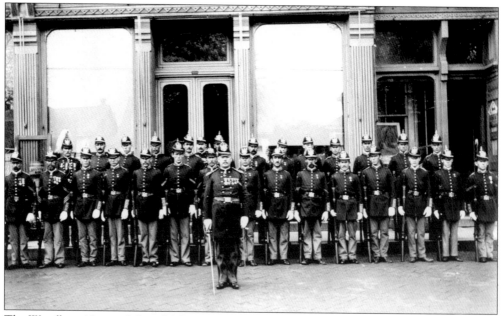

The Woodbury National Guard 6th Regiment posed in 1897 in front of Green's Opera House on the southeast corner of Broad and Centre Streets. Maj. C. Walter Shivers joined the regiment in Woodbury in 1891 when Capt. Edmund DuBois was commanding officer and Col. Daniel Mathers was a second lieutenant. The company performed drills on the third floor. Captain Green bought their uniforms, equipment, and rifles.

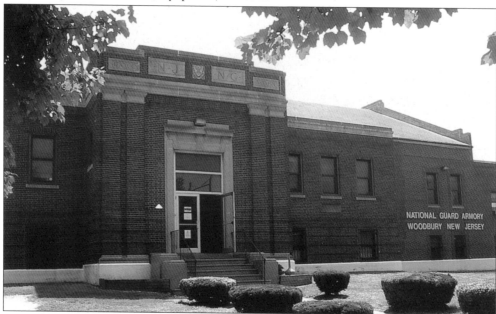

On April 4, 1931, the 3rd Battalion, 114th Infantry dedicated the armory on the northeast corner of Red Bank and Evergreen Avenues with a parade and appropriate exercises. The Woodbury Armory was built as a Works Progress Administration (WPA) project for approximately $75,000. The brick building included an ample drill shed, modern steel lockers, and large storeroom facilities. During the 1950s, the Underwood Hospital Ball was held in this facility.

Four

SCHOOLS

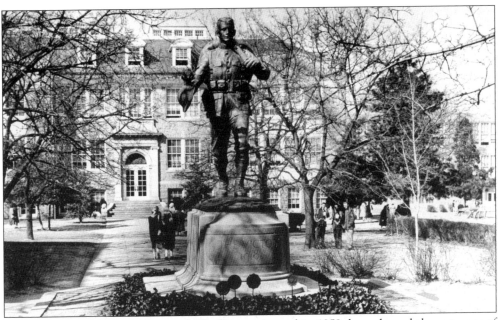

Woodbury's World War I Memorial *The Victor*, pictured in 1958, has adorned the entrance of Woodbury High School since being unveiled and dedicated on Memorial Day, May 30, 1925. In 1921, the Daughters of the American Revolution and the American Legion, along with various Woodbury civic associations, spearheaded a monumental fund-raising drive to establish a perpetual reminder of the sacrifices of war for generations to come. A total of $6,500 was realized from various organizations as well as from residents of Woodbury. After three years of planning, the board of education gave permission for the memorial to be placed on the high school lawn. The bronze, eight-foot, youthful soldier, in full stride, is depicted returning triumphantly from war with a token of victory in his hand. The blanket roll, wrapped leggings, steel helmet, field shoes, and rifle with fixed bayonet are shown with striking clearness. The doughboy was sculptured by internationally known sculptor R. Tait McKenzie and was modeled after Rae "Mugs" McGraw, a "typical American youth." The monument was restored and rededicated in 1994.

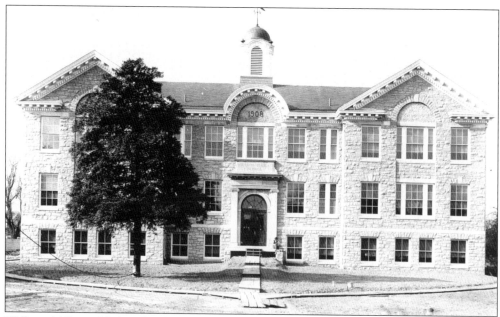

William Milligan High School, named for one of the city's best-known educators, is pictured nearly completed in the fall of 1909. Prior to 1899, the 10th grade was the highest in Woodbury's school system. The contract for the new building was awarded to Joseph Steelman of Bridgeton, New Jersey, for $53,000, but with the furnishings, land, and other equipment, the building would cost almost twice as much.

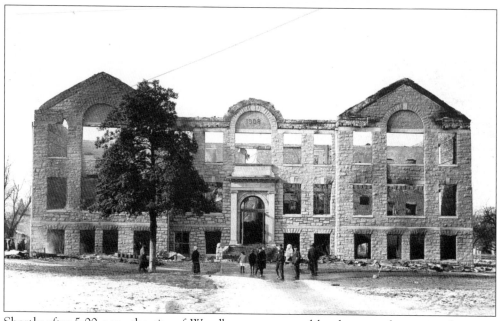

Shortly after 5:00 a.m., the city of Woodbury was ravaged by the most destructive fire in its history according to the *Woodbury Constitution* of December 31, 1910. The cause of the fire at the Milligan High School that morning was shrouded in mystery, although neighbors heard several explosions prior to the first alarm being sounded. Insufficient water pressure seemed to be a large factor in the resulting destruction.

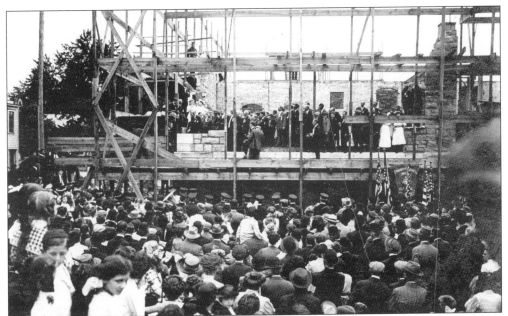

On September 23, 1911, Gov. Woodrow Wilson laid the cornerstone for the soon-to-be-refurbished Woodbury High School. The governor was met at the railroad station by a large delegation of mechanics and city and county officials. The Moose Band led the procession up Cooper Street to the school building. Wilson pronounced the school "the bulwark of the nation and condemned the ideas of some who opposed education."

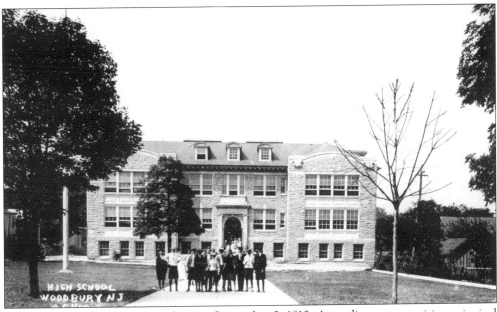

The school reopened with grandeur on September 3, 1912. According to supervising principal Harry Dixon, as noted in the *Woodbury Times* of September 4, "the pupils are more than pleased with their new home." There were 259 high school pupils present on the opening day with more to report later. Male students, wearing knickers, stand proudly in this *c.* 1919 picture in front of Woodbury High School on Broad Street.

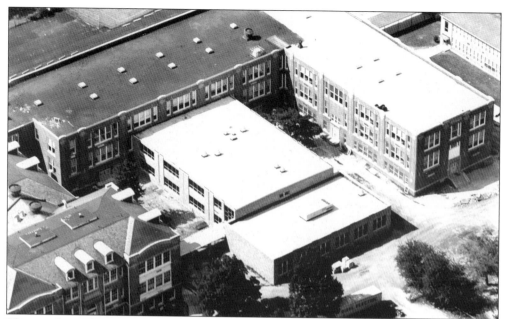

This aerial view depicts a "cluster of impressive buildings," which are, from left to right, Woodbury High School, Woodbury Junior High, and a grade school, during construction of the new library in 1969. In May 1974, the board of education unanimously decided that the gymnasium (top right) officially would be called the Cap Paine Memorial Gym.

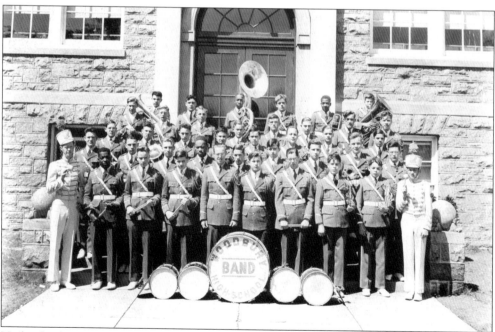

Under the direction of Edward Byerly, the Woodbury High School Band proudly stands in front of the high school in this 1941 picture. Band was made an accredited subject when two periods a week were spent by members rehearsing for competition, shows, and football games during the school year.

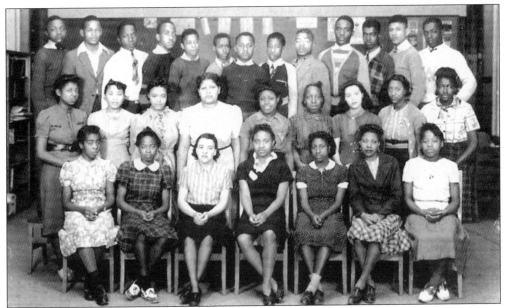

Helen Klepfer was commended for assembling this group of students, pictured in 1940, to continue the vocal tradition of their forefathers. Organized in 1939, this Spiritual Chorus at Woodbury High School was a unique gathering of African American students. In their repertoire were compositions of many types, not simply beautiful spirituals.

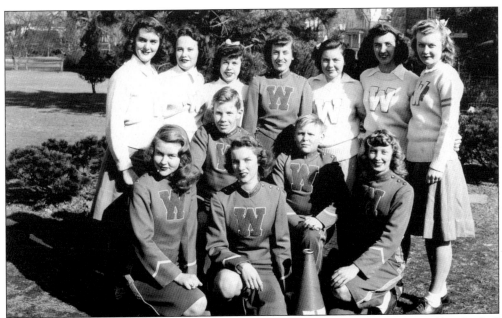

This 1943–1944 Woodbury High School cheerleading squad made a name for itself at football games. Pictured from left to right are (first row) Judy Black (Wellons), Betty Sutton (McLeod), and Janet Bowers (Danse); (second row) Donald Sparks and Ted Moss; (third row) Elizabeth Claypoole (Herr), Ruth Hutton, Jeannette Spicer, Shirley Thompson, Jeanne Burnette (Hagerman), Elsie DuBois (Pratt), and Dorothy Sellen.

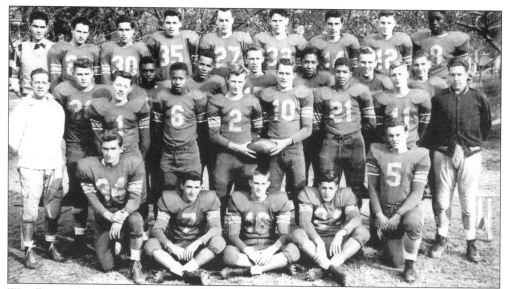

Woodbury High's 1952 varsity football team, coached by Tom "Speedy" Williamson and Mark Wayne, captured three titles that year by defeating rival Paulsboro on November 15 with a 14-0 win. Woodbury's Thundering Herd clinched the Colonial Conference and Gloucester County titles, as well as a clear claim to the SJ Group III title. This allowed the school to enjoy its most successful season with an 8-0 record and 236 points.

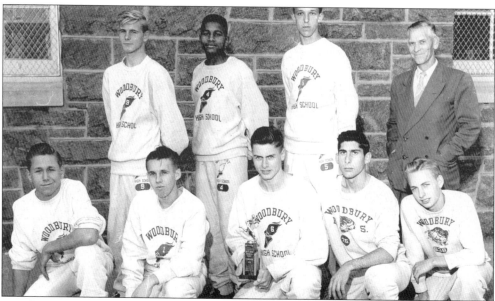

Woodbury's Cross County Team of 1954 experienced another tremendous season that fall, winning eight meets and losing only one. Runners also extended their winning streak to 24 straight, including their third consecutive South Jersey Championship. Pictured from left to right are (first row) A. J. "Berky" Turner, Dick Gardiner, Jim Shea, Lou Coccolone, and Tom McKenna; (second row) Fred Leiby, Carl Hawkins, Dick Hill, and Charles "Cap" Paine (coach).

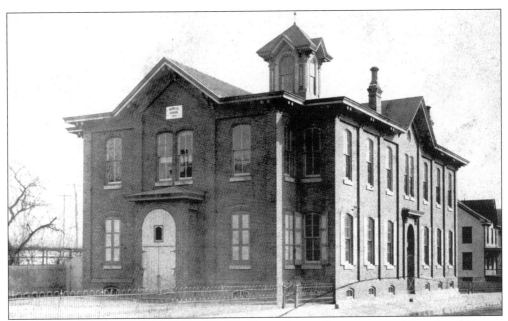

The Woodbury Academy, pictured around 1900 on the northeast corner of Broad and Centre Streets, stood from 1879 until it was demolished in 1925. Land was deeded in 1791 to construct the original building for which Rev. Andrew Hunter Jr. became the first principal. That structure was declared inadequate and was demolished in 1879. The academy educated such prominent men as Capt. James Lawrence, Stephen Decatur, and Benjamin Cooper.

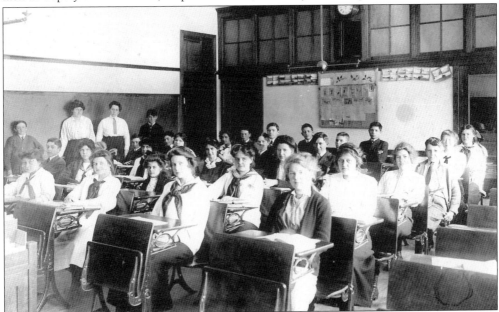

Students of the Woodbury Academy's Room 8A pose in this 1914 picture. By 1920, the board of education realized this structure had become a safety hazard and sold the property at auction. In 1924, construction of the junior high school wing was completed to accommodate the overflow and the growing student population. Sen. Robert Hendrickson, seen seated in the far rear left corner, was another of the academy's alumni.

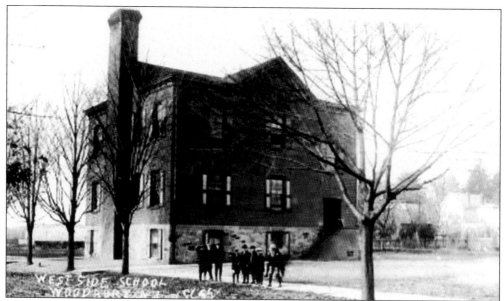

Construction began on the old West End and Walnut Street Schools in 1889 with four rooms each and each costing $12,755. Old West End School, pictured around 1900, was on the northeast corner of Penn and Glover Streets. When the school opened, the children marched from the Old Academy to West End where Ray Paulin later served as principal. The old school now houses the Sketch Club Players.

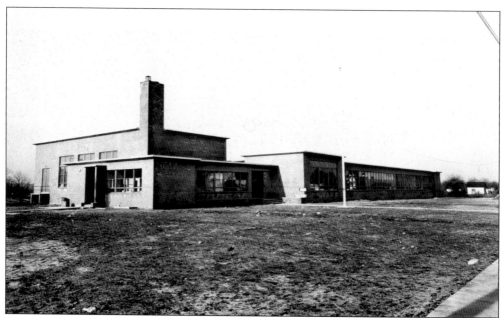

Construction on the new West End School on South Jackson Street began in 1949. Seen here in 1950 before completion, this $400,000, nine-classroom building housed an auditorium, library, offices, and kitchen for kindergarten through eighth grade. Dedicatory services in March of that year included an address by U.S. senator Hon. Robert C. Hendrickson and the national anthem led by Helen Klepfer, director of vocal music at Woodbury High School.

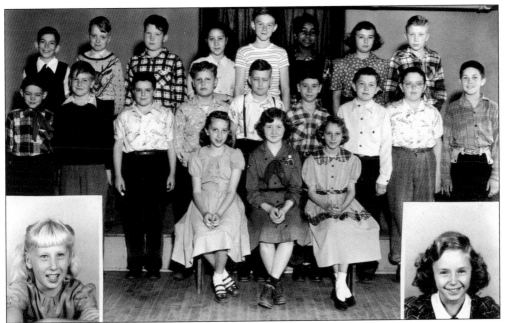

Members of Walnut Street School's 1950 sixth-grade class are, from left to right, (insets) JoAnn Kramer and Nancy Harker; (first row) Judy Clark, Ruth Anne Renner, and Barbara Burtch; (second row) Ken Vaneman, Wayne Seher, Howard Gwin, Dave Reinmuth, James Berger, Dale Niedt, Bobby Wilgus, Herbert Lancaster, and Don Layton; (third row) Charles Rapp, Richard Wolfrom, Davis Harold, Rosemarie Russo, Richard Roll, Gail Wagner, Joan Pedrick, and Robert Barr.

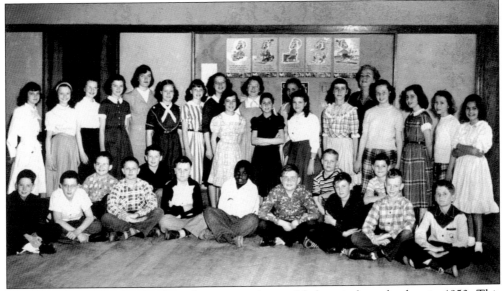

Bessie Beatty, Central School teacher, is seen here with her sixth-grade class in 1950. This class would later become the Woodbury High School graduating class of 1957. Central School, dedicated in October 1924, became Woodbury's newest grammar school. The L-shaped building, constructed at an approximate cost of $450,000, housed a gymnasium, an 860-seat auditorium, and over 25 classrooms. It was used by grades kindergarten through eight.

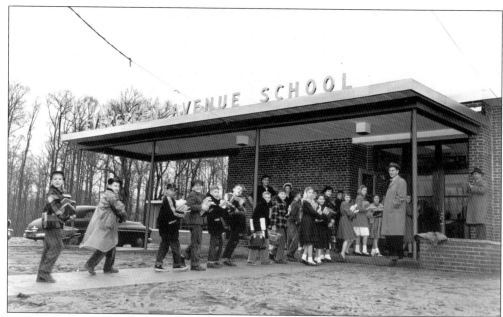

On December 22, 1953, pupils marched to their new $330,000 Evergreen Avenue School for a get-acquainted time after being temporarily housed in the Central and Walnut Street Schools. The building was officially opened on January 4, 1954, with an enrollment of 351 students with Grace Emrich as head teacher. Participating in the activities, standing on the far right, are Warren McClain, superintendent, and John Stouffer, elementary supervisor.

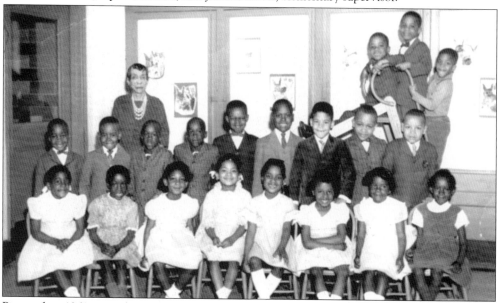

Pictured in 1961 is teaching principal Harriet Sturges's kindergarten class at Carpenter Street School. The school began in 1840 for African American children as a segregated two-room wooden structure near Bethel African Methodist Episcopal Church. In 1889, another school was constructed and used until the board of education took steps to integrate children and teachers in September 1963. The school was abandoned in 1964, and the building was taken over by the county.

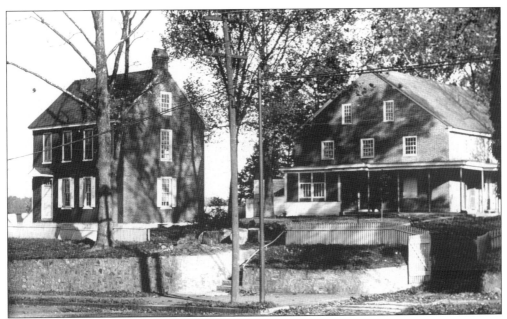

As early as 1773, the Woodbury Friends Meeting began their school in Woodbury. A committee was appointed in 1811 to construct a two-story brick schoolhouse on the meetinghouse lot. This school, pictured around 1895, was first used for the instruction of females in writing, arithmetic, sewing, and reading and was maintained by the Friends for almost a century. This building was torn down in 1926.

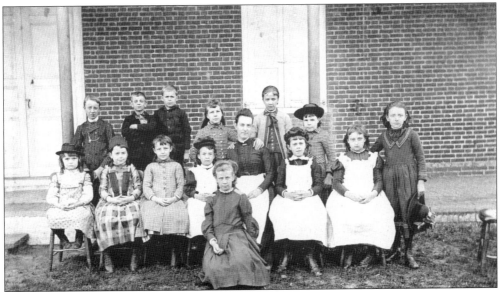

These children from the Friends School on North Broad Street posed around 1888 for a picture with their teacher. The Friends School welcomed students of any religious persuasion. In September 1952, the school was reinstituted with a new structure at the same location and operated continuously until the doors were closed in June 1970.

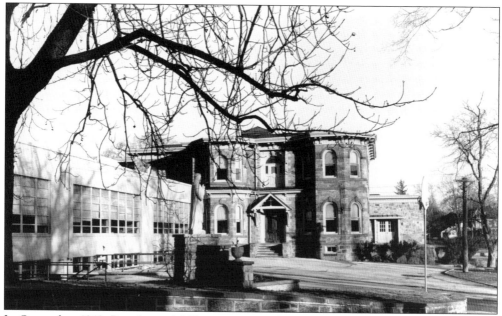

In September 1943, Rev. James McKeever, pastor of St. Patrick's Church, purchased Colonel Greene's eight-acre estate on the southeast corner of Green and Cooper Streets for a parochial school. In October 1944, St. Patrick's school began with 61 students in kindergarten through third grade with Sister Margaret as the first principal. Two years after this picture, fire ravaged the old Green mansion in 1968, destroying the library and one classroom.

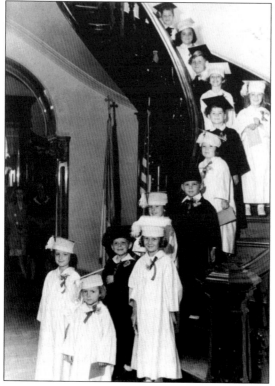

Students of St. Patrick's kindergarten graduating class of June 13, 1947, are, from front to back, Judy Beckett, Dorothy Gallagher, Mary Lou Smith, Mike Burns, Barbara Batten, Joseph DiMartini, Amber Muller, Robert Held, Veronica Keebler, Pat Yearicks, William Riley, Roseann Angelastro, and Michael Bartie.

Five

CHURCHES

Woodbury was settled on the conviction of religious freedom. When the Wood family was forced to leave their home in Bury, Lancashire, England, because of their doctrinal practices of the Quaker religion, they came to America to seek that freedom. Today the many houses of worship in the city reflect that diversity of religious freedom that brought believers to this country. This postcard shows the doors of the churches of Woodbury, which architecturally have adorned the city's landscape with splendor and grace for generations. From left to right are (first row) Christ Episcopal Church and the Presbyterian Church at Woodbury; (second row) St. Patrick's Roman Catholic Church and Kemble Memorial United Methodist Church.

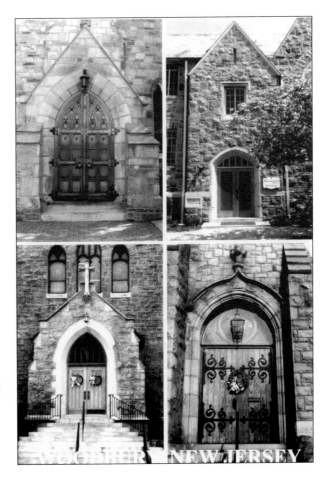

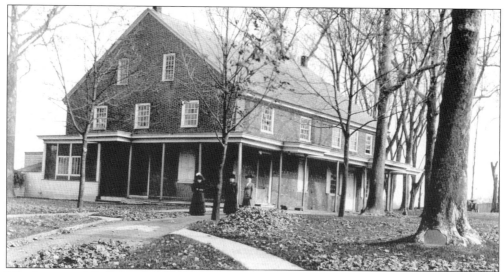

The Society of Friends Meeting House, located on the northeast side of North Broad and Hunter Streets, was constructed in the fall of 1715. John Cooper, a man of much influence in the community, was the builder of the red and blue brick building. Pictured in this *c.* 1900 photograph, from left to right, are Marie Clement, Alice David, and Sybil Tatum Jones.

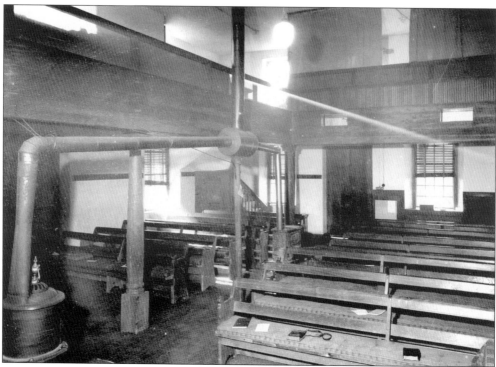

This interior view of the east side of the Society of Friends Meeting House was taken before the stoves were removed during the winter of 1951. This house of worship is an example of true simplicity with plain paneling, wide beam wooden floors, and sturdy handmade wooden benches. In the early days, men sat on one side of the aisle while the women were on the other side during worship.

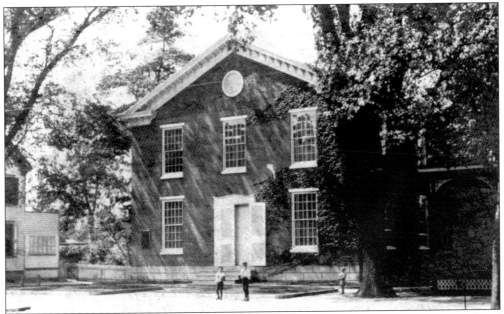

The Presbyterian Church at Woodbury, pictured in 1890 on the northwest corner of Broad and Centre Streets, was constructed in 1834. When Woodbury was still a wilderness, 10 Presbyterian families met in a log structure located near the present Presbyterian Cemetery on North Broad Street. In 1906, extensive renovations were made to the building, including a bell tower and a stone facade, which were both removed by 1971.

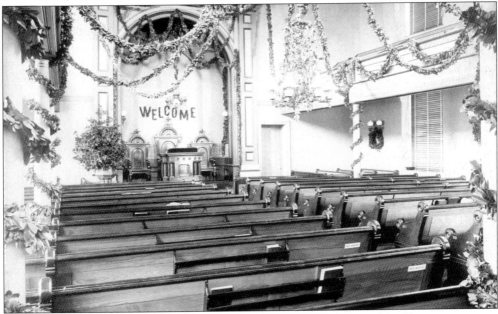

This c. 1900 interior view of the Presbyterian church sanctuary, decorated for Christmas, appears much the same way as it did when constructed. In 1906, during the pastorate of Rev. George Tomson, the sanctuary was enlarged 16 feet to the rear, allowing for additional pews. At this time, a pipe organ was installed, which graced the front of the sanctuary. The church was simultaneously wired for electricity.

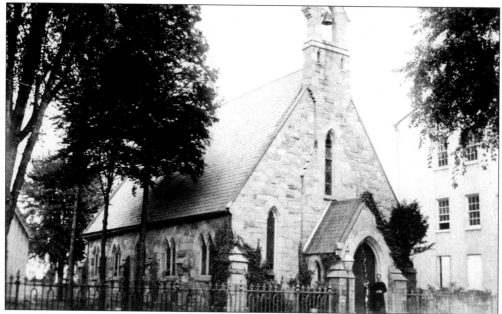

Christ Episcopal Church is seen here around 1880. Located at Delaware and New Streets, it was constructed in 1856. Worship services began in 1815 when either the bishop or priests from Clarksboro and Chew's Landing conducted services. By 1854, regular services commenced with the appointment of Rev. William Herbert Norris. The property was purchased in 1855, and construction began. Bishop Doane consecrated the church in 1857.

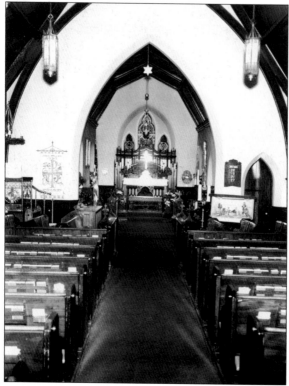

The interior of Christ Church is seen as it appeared at Christmas 1966. During the pastorate of Rev. Howard E. Thompson, the church excelled in growth and spiritual guidance. In 1911, a fire, which started in the basement, caused much damage to the altar area. Women of the church rushed in to retrieve the altar cloth, Bible, and bishop's chair. A new parish hall was constructed in 1914.

Kemble Memorial Methodist Episcopal Church, located at 19 South Broad Street, is pictured around 1900. Hazelhurst and Huckel, the same architects responsible for the Gloucester County Courthouse, designed it. William Kemble of Philadelphia donated money for the present structure in 1888 in honor of his mother, Elizabeth. The congregation was responsible for only $15,000 of the $120,000 cost. The edifice was dedicated on February 22, 1891.

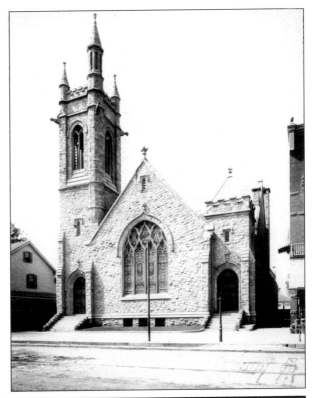

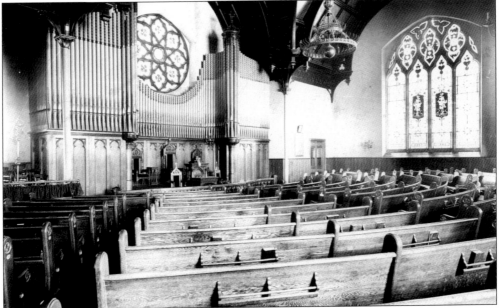

In 1902, the members of Kemble Memorial Methodist Episcopal Church purchased a new pipe organ from W. W. Kimball Organ Company of Chicago at a cost of $3,600. Due to increased enrollment in 1928, an education building was constructed to the rear of the original edifice. In 1949, the sanctuary's interior was renovated, and a new organ, tower chimes, and chancel were installed for a cost of $37,000.

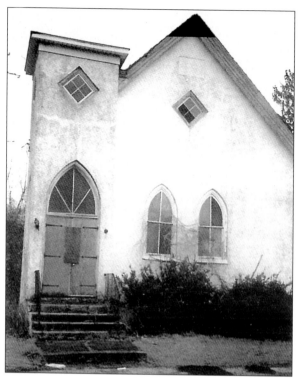

Bethel African Methodist Episcopal Church began when five inspired women each gave $1 to establish a building fund in 1838. This quaint wooden structure, located on Haytean Street (Carpenter Street), was consecrated on November 1, 1840. The church was rebuilt under the pastorate of Rev. Robert Turner in 1874. This picture was taken after the congregation moved into a new church in 1981. The church was demolished in March 1994.

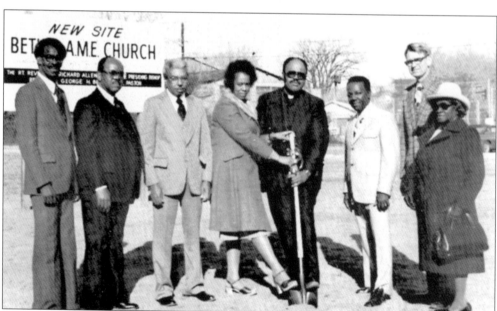

Groundbreaking ceremonies were held in 1980 for the new Bethel African Methodist Episcopal Church on Courtland Street. Due to the interest in Christian education and spiritual growth, Pastor George Beachum revived a dream in 1977 by establishing a building committee to evaluate the possibility of building a new church. Pictured from left to right are Roland Williams, Eugene Kirby, Clarence Harwell, Anita Heard, Reverend Beachum, John Wilson, Ernest Hoh, and Anna Sye.

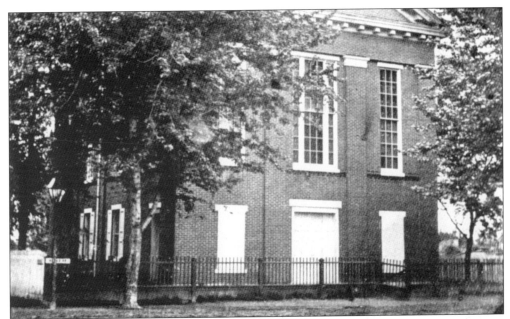

The First Baptist Church of Woodbury, pictured in 1876, was constructed for a cost of $600 in 1858. Located at North Broad and Packer Streets, members met in 1857 to formulate plans to build a house of worship. Around 1912, millionaire-tycoon Andrew Carnegie donated an organ to the congregation. In 1957, construction for a new sanctuary began adjacent to the original building and was completed in 1958.

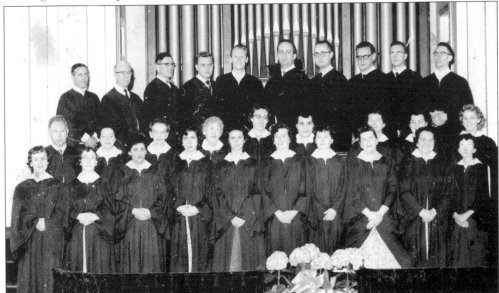

Members of the First Baptist Church choir of 1957 are (first row) Ruth Doty, Florence Kelsey, Shirley Everingham, Beth Clemens, Marie Wiegand, Lucille Sgorlon, Claire Sweeten, Eleanor Hobbs, Mildred Side, and Emma King; (second row) Arleigh Clemens, Lila Jefferys, Katherine Lang, Edythe Holloway, Grace Janson, Florence Simpkins, Catherine Kipp, and Gladys Megary; (third row) John Collier, Percival Lang, Bob Morrison, Jim Berger, Nelson Palmer, Warren Kipp, Phillip Spaeth, Tony Hampel, Al Sarfert, and Donald Frazier.

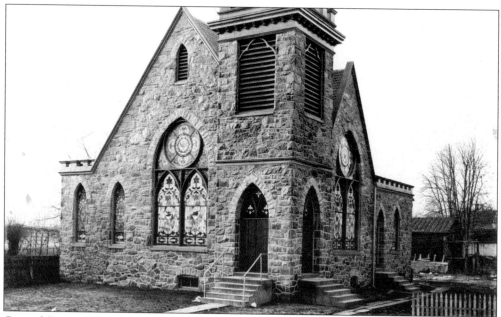

Central Baptist Church, constructed at a cost of $6,250 in 1903, was located on East Centre Street behind the Green Building. After receiving letters of dismission from the First Baptist Church, this congregation was formed. The cornerstone was laid with appropriate exercises in May 1902 and dedicated in June 1903. Upon outgrowing this facility, the congregation moved to its present location in 1951. The old church was sold and demolished.

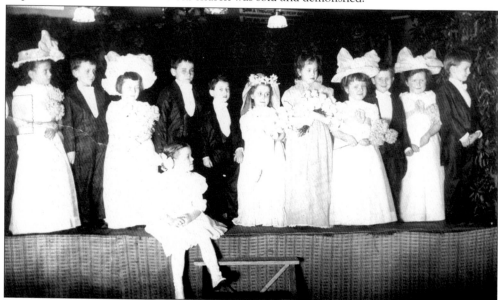

This Tom Thumb wedding was held in the Central Baptist Church around 1908. Charles Stratton, also known as Tom Thumb, was a 35-inch-tall man who teamed up with showman Phineas T. Barnum of Barnum and Bailey Circus. Later Tom Thumb weddings using children were popular fund-raisers. Pictured from left to right are Pauline Albright, unidentified, Elizabeth Clark, Dan Mumford, Edward Talman, Marion Thoman, Ruth Woolley, Harriet Holdstein, Josiah Park, Emma Holdstein, and Samuel Ross. Seated is Helen Redfield.

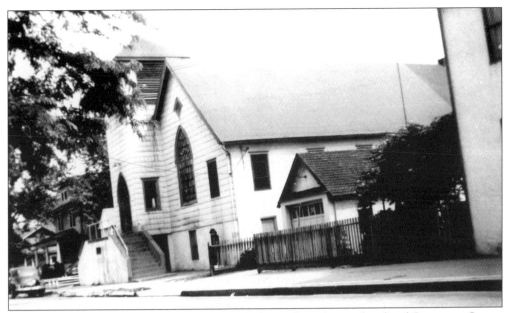

Pictured in 1954 is Bethlehem Baptist Church, located on the south side of Carpenter Street. The church was chartered in 1896 by seven people while meeting in various members' homes. In 1906, during the pastorate of Rev. Stephen Harris, a church building was constructed at a cost of $2,300 and dedicated in April 1907. Before being torn down in 2002, this building was used as the Woodbury Child Development Center.

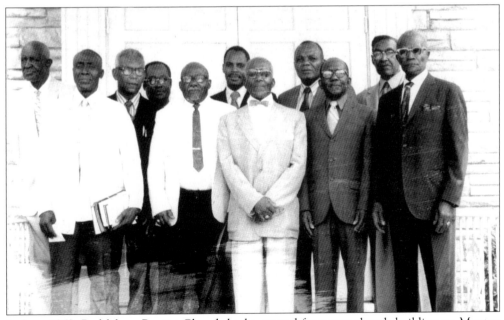

In June 1962, Bethlehem Baptist Church broke ground for a new church building on Mantua Avenue. Trustees and deacons of the Bethlehem Baptist Church pose in front of their church in 1971. Pictured from left to right are Ernest Carter, George Bagby, James Waugh, Hugh Ellis, James Coleman, Rev. Vincent Cream, Archie Bagby, Arnold Cream ("Jersey Joe Walcott"), Haskell Hampton, Lawrence Triplett, and Edward Jordan.

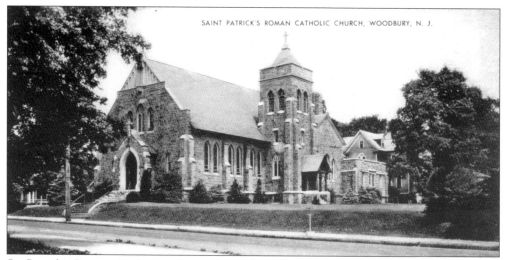

St. Patrick's Roman Catholic Church, located on the northeast side of Cooper and Euclid Streets, was built in 1909 at a cost of $19,060. The first account of services held in Woodbury was recorded in 1793. A mission church was established, and in 1865, Old Saint Patrick's Church on Salem Avenue was constructed. A parish was established in 1877 with Rev. M. A. McManus as pastor.

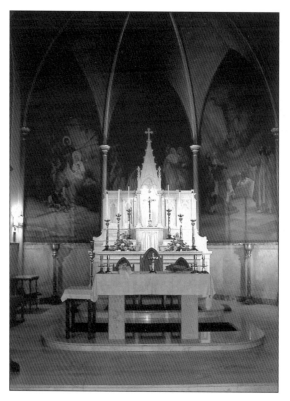

This interior view of St. Patrick's Church illustrates the magnificent architecture after the 1924 renovations when a marble high altar was erected. Shortly thereafter, the marble side altars and stained-glass windows were added to the sanctuary. Extensive renovations were also made in 1923, enlarging the seating capacity to 200 at a cost of $40,000. In 1927, marble was placed throughout the sanctuary along with additional stained-glass windows.

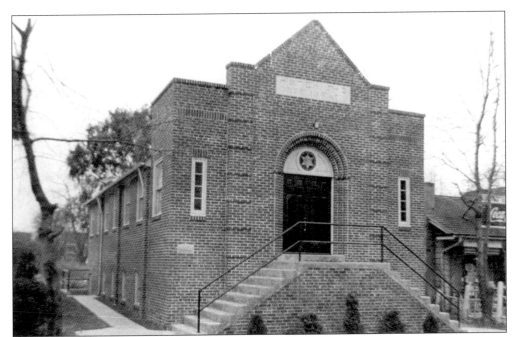

Fourteen families met in 1922 to establish a synagogue in Woodbury. By 1923, services were being held in the old Academy School, located at the northeast corner of Broad and East Centre Streets, for the high holy days. In 1937, land for a permanent synagogue was purchased at 57 West Center Street and with a membership of only 22, a synagogue was constructed for $7,500.

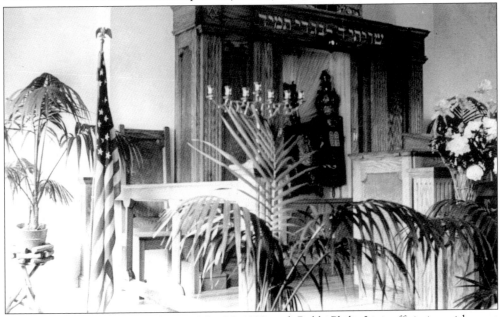

Dedication ceremonies took place on May 28, 1939, with Rabbi Philip Lipis officiating with guest speakers Mayor Joseph Bauer, Hugh Mehorter, and Judge John Boyd Avis. The congregation purchased its first Torah, the holy scrolls, which were housed in the ark. The honor of the dedication of Torah was given to Harry Polsky and Harry Bleznak. The present synagogue, located at High and Warner Streets, was dedicated in 1962.

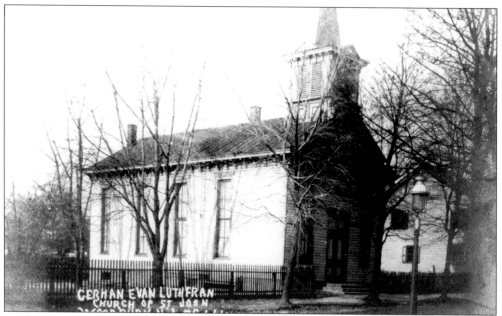

The German Evangelical Lutheran Church of St. John, pictured around 1910, was built in 1884. A parcel of land was purchased in 1883 from John Tatum at Lincoln and Salem Avenues for the site of a new church. This congregation, known as the German Presbyterian Church, was organized in May 1882. In February 1887, they transferred their allegiance to the German Lutheran Synod. The church was razed in 1967.

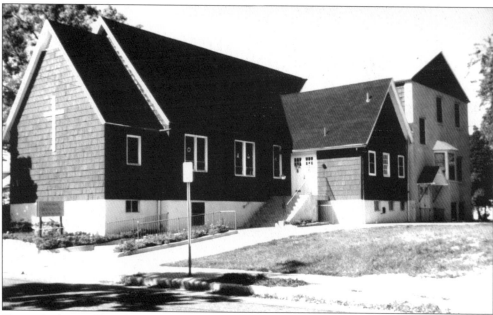

Trinity Lutheran Church, pictured in 1983, was built on a lot donated by Frank and Leon Budd at 64 Progress Avenue. In 1923, plans were formulated to build a church, and the church was completed in September 1926. On March 27, 1966, St. John's and Trinity Lutheran Church merged to form St. Stephen's Lutheran Church. Their present edifice on North Evergreen Avenue was built at a cost of $750,000.

Six

NEIGHBORHOODS

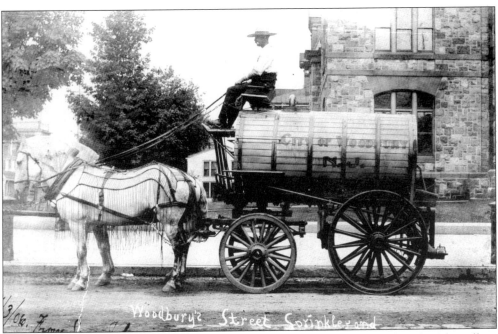

The trials encountered in travel made the early citizens of Woodbury realize that the village needed roads to survive. Several of the old Native American trails passed through Woodbury, and the pioneers usually took advantage of these and built their roads upon them. Because of the dirt roads, they were a perfect bed of dust during dry and hot seasons. In July 1878, a number of citizens urged the sprinkling of Broad Street, and the residents were asked to contribute money to cover the costs. In 1879, the residents of Broad Street refused to guarantee enough money. When the sprinkler did run, as in this 1906 picture, the dust was too thick for it to make much headway. The opposite occurred during inclement weather, which caused muddy streets. Someone penned the following to show his true feelings about the dusty streets. "How does the little sprinkling cart improve the dusty streets, and scatters little drops of wet on everyone it meets?"

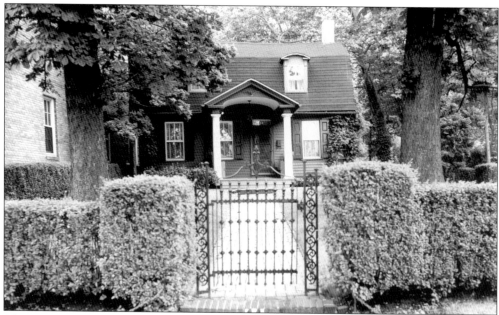

This 1911 picture is of the Franklin House at 44 North Broad Street, the oldest house in Woodbury. Built prior to 1765, it was purchased in 1823 by Hon. Joseph Franklin and remained in the Franklin family until 1911. One original fireplace still displays the square handmade bricks. In the 1950s, Dr. John Stouffer lived there, and more recently Phyllis Raynor Kidder has owned the house.

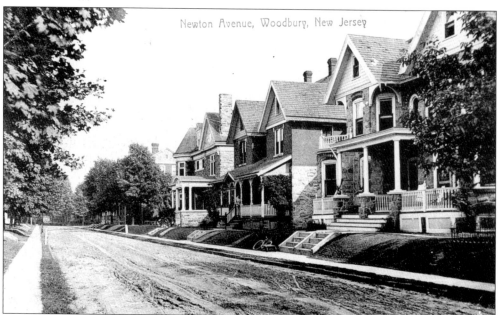

Newton Avenue, Woodbury, New Jersey

After purchasing and refurbishing the Newton Hotel, Mahlon Newton directed his attention to real estate ventures. After Newton established Curtis Avenue, he turned his attention to developing Newton Avenue and built several more houses. Shown in this 1908 photograph is the south side of Newton Avenue. The third house (right), built in 1893, was the home of Edward Bradway in 1924 and was later owned by pediatrician Dr. Paul Pegau.

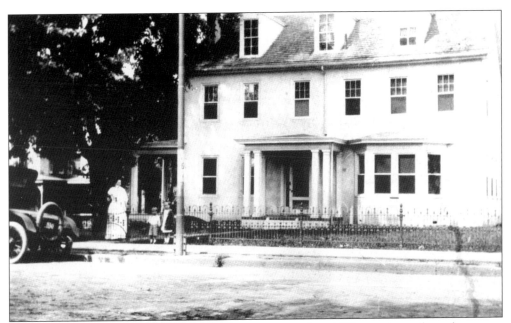

Dr. J. Harris Underwood's home, pictured as it appeared in 1920, was located on the corner of North Broad Street and West Red Bank Avenue. Sarah Cliver Underwood, J. Harris's wife, is pictured with her nephew, Harris Willet, and her daughter, Dorothy Underwood (Livezey). J. Harris and his brother, Amos, began their medical and dental practice on the first floor of this building. The home was razed around 1972 for hospital parking.

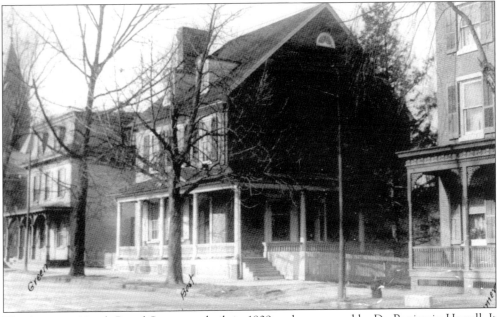

This home on North Broad Street was built in 1809 and was owned by Dr. Benjamin Howell. It was later purchased by the Matlock sisters who contracted to have the house taken down piece by piece and rebuilt on its present site at 34 Hunter Street. The McGuinness Funeral Home was established there in 1950. The original house site is now occupied by the Woodbury Post Office.

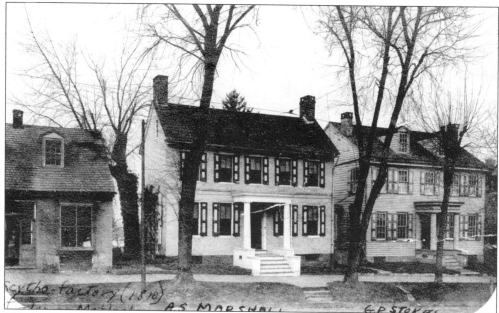

The former Gloucester County YMCA building, seen around 1890 on the far right, stood across from the Friends Meeting House on Broad Street. The YMCA used this building from 1926 until the early 1960s. The structure was later torn down. The Alfred S. Marshall house (center) was eventually owned by Dr. Ralph Moore and now houses a medical office. An old scythe shop is on the left.

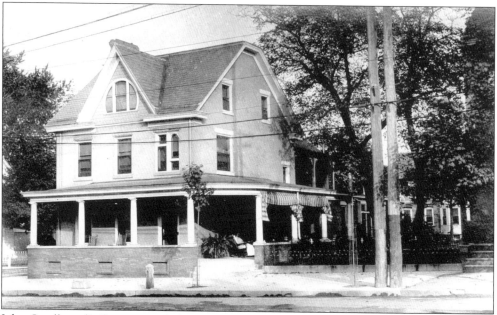

John Smallwood's Georgian-style home, pictured around 1900, was built in the late 1760s on the southeast corner of Broad Street and Newton Avenue. David Watkins, who was elected acting governor of New Jersey in 1899, resided here until his death in 1938. His stepdaughter, Virginia Andrews, lived here until her death in 1957 when the property was sold to the board of education. The building was razed in 1970.

96

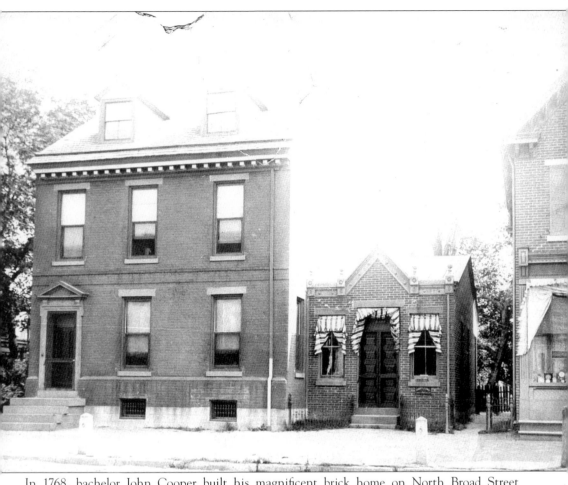

In 1768, bachelor John Cooper built his magnificent brick home on North Broad Street between Cooper Street and Newton Avenue. When the British came to Woodbury during the Revolutionary War in 1777, Cooper was forced to flee because of his prominence as a patriot. Cooper locked his silver in a closet before escaping to the home of his sister, Ann Whitall. When Lord Charles Cornwallis came into the village, he chose the finest mansion to serve as his headquarters. Cornwallis seized and occupied the Cooper home from November 21 to 23. During the stay, his subalterns amused themselves by prying open the closets with their bayonets. The marks from Cornwallis's men remained until the day the house was torn down in 1971. Dr. Joseph Hughes occupied the house and attached office during the late 1940s and early 1950s. The Gloucester County Historical Society saved the second-floor fireplace wall and installed it in their new library in 1973. The building on the right was Porter's Jewelry Store and later the home and office of city treasurer and lawyer Ernest Redfield.

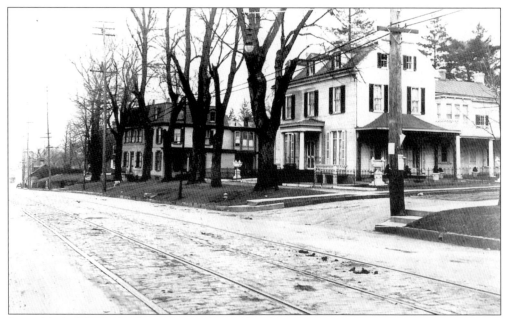

James Matlock built this home at North Broad and Hunter Streets in 1833. Dr. William Brewer converted the building into a hospital in 1919. The structure was later demolished in 1958. To the left is Michael Fisher's house, which was built in 1763. This later became the Lydia Paul property, which the Gloucester County Historical Society purchased in 1912 for $2,000. The society occupied this building until 1923.

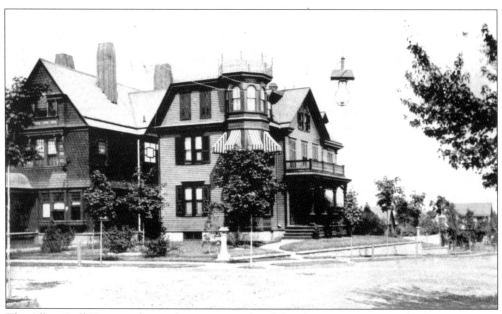

The Albert Dell House at the northeast corner of Euclid and Hunter Streets was built around 1890. This c. 1910 picture of the three-story Queen Anne–style frame building features a cross-gabled roof, a corner tower, and gabled dormers. Today this is the home of the Homestead Title Agency.

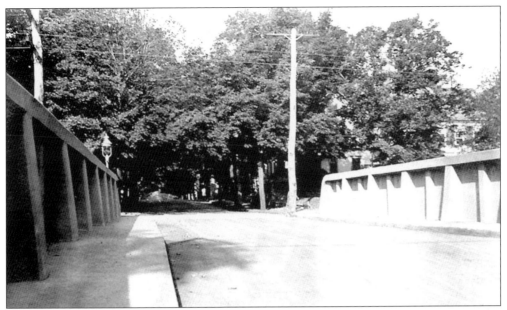

Hunter Street was named in honor of Rev. Andrew Hunter, Presbyterian clergyman and a tea burner of the Greenwich Tea Party in 1774. In 1878, an iron bridge was constructed over the railroad allowing for a viable thoroughfare between Evergreen Avenue and Broad Street. Later refurbished to concrete, the bridge, pictured around 1922, was sometimes closed during snowstorms in the 1950s, allowing local children to sled down the steep incline.

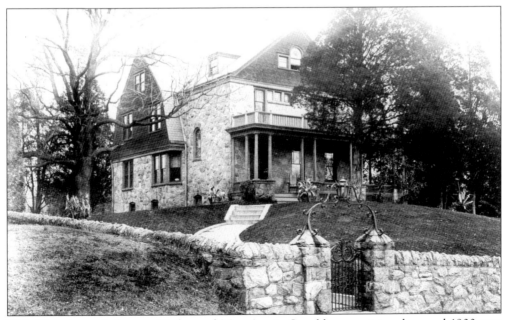

This Victorian-style home of Judge and Mrs. Austin Swackhamer, pictured around 1900, was built in 1888 by George Barker. Overlooking Stewart Lake, it features rough-cut stone on the first story and a half, with contrasting stone sills and lintels. During the 1950s, their son, Donald, a well-known attorney in Woodbury with offices on Cooper Street, made this his home until his death in 1959.

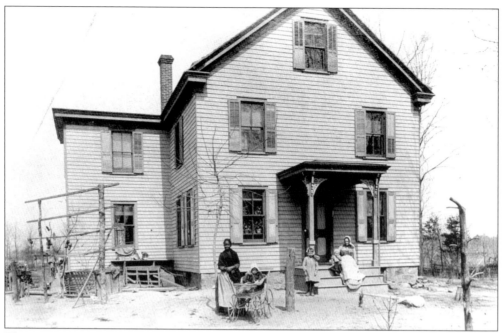

This *c.* 1893 picture shows the Andes and Emma Budd homestead at 157 Hessian Avenue, which is now located in West Deptford Township. One of their children pictured is possibly Leon or Frank. Their nanny is standing (left) while Emma is seated on the porch. All of the Budd children were born while the family resided here. During the 1920s, their sons Frank, Leon, and Charles developed much of North Woodbury.

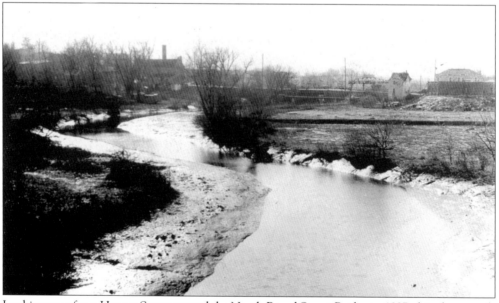

Looking west from Hunter Street toward the North Broad Street Bridge in 1927, this photograph shows the original Woodbury Lake system. In 1935, prominent historian Frank Stewart urged the city to seek a WPA grant for construction of what would become a planned chain of lakes and parks in the city. The Underwood Hospital parking lot now stands on the far right with the police station on the left of the waterway.

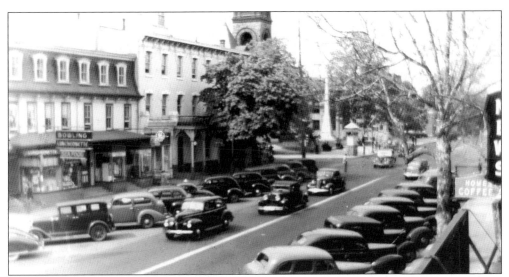

In this 1940 northward view of Broad and Delaware Streets, traffic seems as busy then as it is now. The traffic control booth, noticeable on the corner, was necessary prior to signal lights being installed to control the heavy volume. The bowling alley and the Newton Hotel are seen on the west side, while the Homestead Coffee Shop is on the east side.

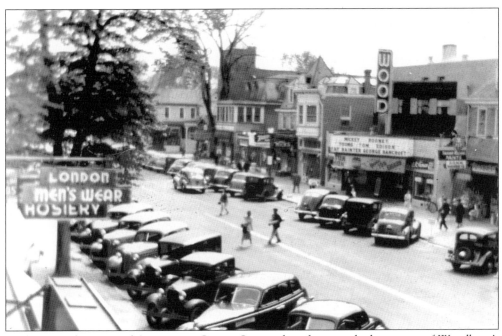

Looking south on Broad Street near Centre Street, this photograph shows part of Woodbury's busy business district in 1940. On Friday and Saturday nights, most stores were open for business, or one could enjoy a movie such as this black-and-white *Young Tom Edison* flick at the Wood Theatre, with Mickey Rooney as Tom, Fay Bainter as Mrs. Samuel (Nancy) Edison, and George Bancroft as Samuel Edison.

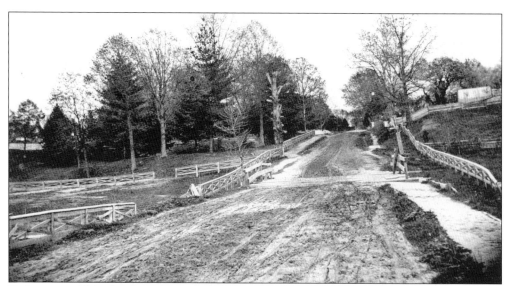

Today it would be hard to imagine not seeing traffic along Cooper Street. Looking east in this *c*. 1876 picture, the Cooper Street Bridge over Hester's Branch was then made of wooden clapboards. The bridge was replaced in 1878 with stone taken from the old jail after it was demolished. Cooper Street was first paved with oyster shells until 1903 when it was then paved with other material.

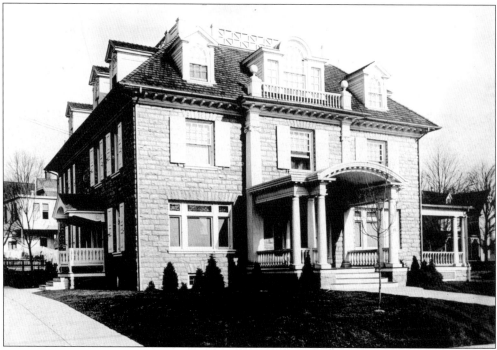

This 1910 picture of the Georgian Revival–style home at 64 Cooper Street was built around 1880 by Daniel Steelman at the time of his marriage. Steelman served for 25 years as Gloucester County superintendent of schools before he died in 1940. During the 1950s, Dr. Baxter Livengood and his family occupied the home before St. Patrick's Church bought the property in 1958 for a rectory.

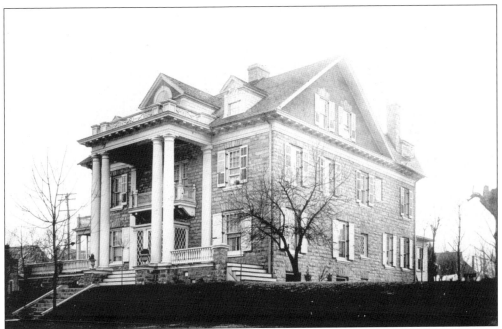

The western side of the Judge Lewis Starr home, built in 1900 on Cooper Street, is depicted here around 1910. This Georgian-style home was designed by Charles Peddle. Judge Starr graduated from the University of Pennsylvania in 1877 and became county prosecutor in 1896. By 1950, this edifice was Clarence Andrew's Funeral Home before Paul Budd opened his funeral business in 1966. Today this home is a private residence.

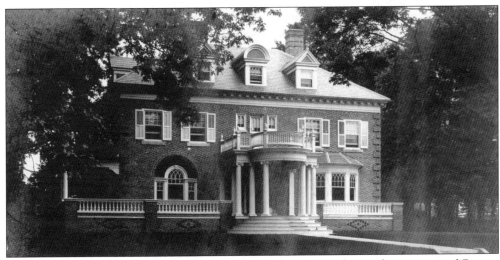

The George Chenowith House, built around 1905, is located on the northeast corner of Cooper Street and Woodland Avenue. This home, pictured around 1910, is known for its large balconied portico in the Doric order with elliptical fanlight and sidelights. In the 1950s, it was the home of the Frank Flowers family.

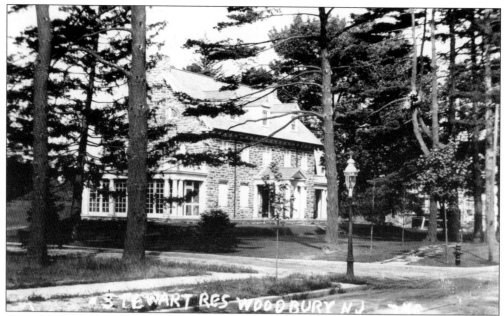

County historian Frank Stewart built this Georgian Revival home in 1914 at the northeast corner of Cooper Street and Rugby Place. The three-story home, known as Rugby Pines, contained eight bedrooms, six baths, a billiard room, and a shuffleboard room. Stewart became president of the Gloucester County Historical Society in 1918. In later years, the Oram Kline and Robert Boakes families resided here. In 2000, Rowan University purchased this home for its president.

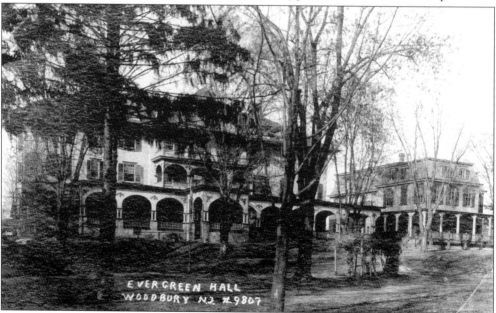

Located on the northeast corner of Cooper Street and Evergreen Avenue, Evergreen Hall, pictured around 1905, was formerly the residence of Edward Hall. In 1885, it was purchased by G. G. Green. After using the home as a boardinghouse for two years, Green thoroughly overhauled and enlarged the edifice, making the house a most desirable resort for summer visitors from Philadelphia. It was destroyed by fire in 1925 and was later rebuilt.

Woodbury's first millionaire, Col. George G. Green, was born in Clarksboro in 1842. After traveling in the Midwest, Green settled in Ohio where he met and married Angie Brown. He later started a retail drug business there in 1869. In November 1872, he settled in Woodbury, purchased an interest in his father's medicine business, and began manufacturing Green's August Flower and Ague Conquerer. Green died in 1925.

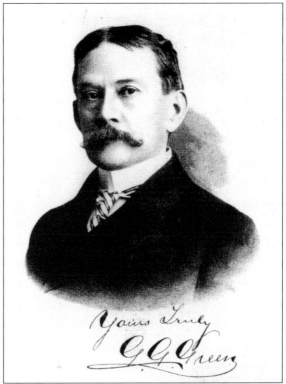

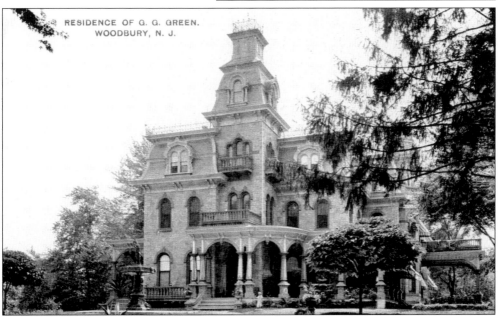

One of Woodbury's stately mansions, Gray Towers, built on Cooper Street in 1889 by George G. Green, was topped with iron-trimmed cupolas, heated by steam, and lighted by gas manufactured on the premises. The interior was finished using exotic woods with gold- and nickel-plate hardware. In 1943, St. Patrick's Parish purchased the building and renovated it as a parochial school before it was ravaged by fire in 1968.

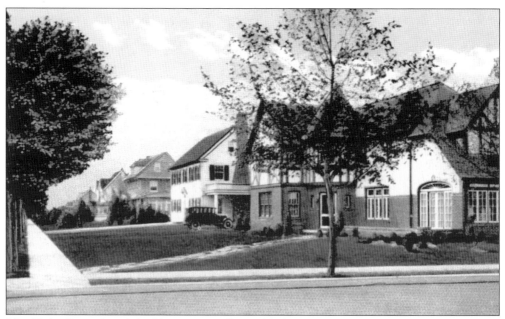

This Tudor Revival–style building, reportedly modeled after Mary Pickford's home in California, is located on the northwest corner of Warner and Delaware Streets. This home, in the Delaware Street District, was built around 1915 by Woodbury's general contractor, John Allen. It is known for its hipped wing roof and gabled dormers with a half-timbered second floor. During the 1950s, attorney Fred Gravino and his family occupied the home.

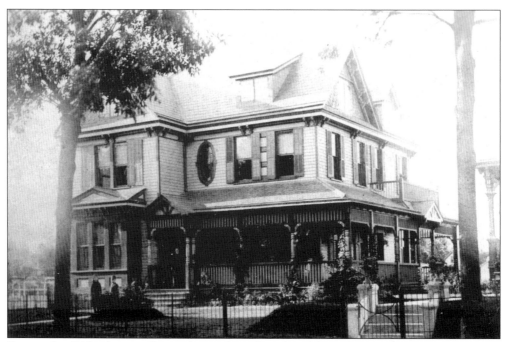

During the 1930s, this was the residence of Josiah and Amelia Dubois. Pictured around 1890, it was built by William Bradway and was located at 61 Delaware Street between Harrison Street and Lupton Avenue. A parking lot encompassed the lot after the house was demolished around 1970.

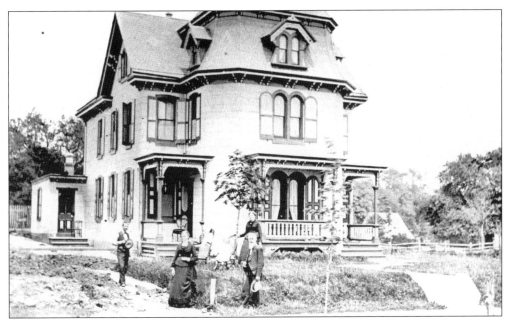

The Henry Clay Foote home at 42 East Centre Street was built in 1876. This Victorian 13-room home, seen here shortly after construction, was in the Foote family for three generations. The residence, pictured around 1880 with a gable and a mansard-roofed bay, was later the home of his daughter, Martha (Mattie) Foote and her husband, Howard Hanthorn. Their son, Horace, continued to live in this home until his death in 1989.

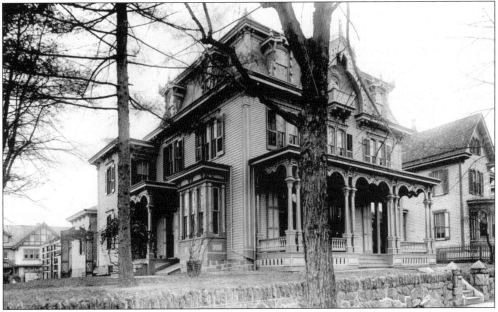

As seen in this undated photograph, the home at 37 East Centre Street was the residence of William Duffield in 1924. In 1982, this Second Empire–style house with mansard roof, central hood mould, and elaborately trimmed dormers was the medical office of Dr. Francis M. Brower III. It was during this time that apartments were located on the upper floors. A magnificent home on Aberdeen Place is seen in the background.

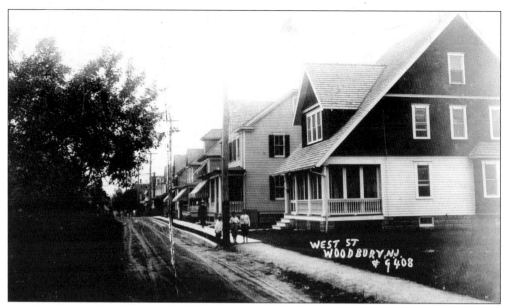

These homes on West Street in 1914 were built before the street was paved. This area, known as the Glover District, represented a residential development for the influx of workers employed at Green's patent medicine laboratory between 1870 and 1890. The West End was laid out by and named for Jacob Glover, a local blacksmith and businessman, whose home and shop were on the corner of High and Broad Streets.

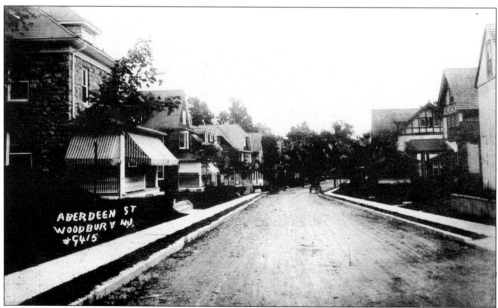

This 1914 picture of Aberdeen Place, located between East Centre and Hopkins Street, depicts the stately homes in the Newton District. This district, developed by Mahlon Newton, derived its significance from the style of brick used on Victorian structures erected between 1880 and 1920. Newton planned and laid out Newton and Curtis Avenues and Aberdeen Place. In the 1950s, the Colbourns, Hannolds, Laubs, Pontons, and Tripleys resided on this street.

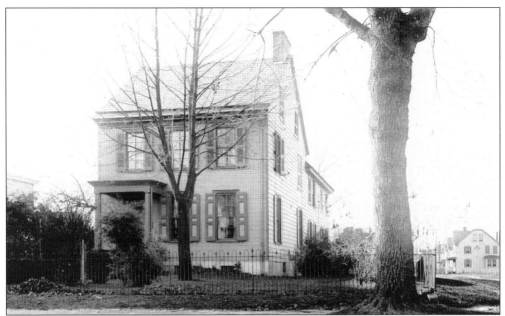

One of Woodbury's oldest homes on the southwest corner of Broad and West Streets was built around 1773. Once known as the Seven Stars Tavern, it became the residence of Joseph Ogden in 1827 and was later renamed Wisteria House. Ogden's great-granddaughter, Sibyl Tatum Jones, lived here before becoming resident curator of the Gloucester County Historical Society. In 1933, the property was sold to William Snelbaker and in 1946 to William Raynor.

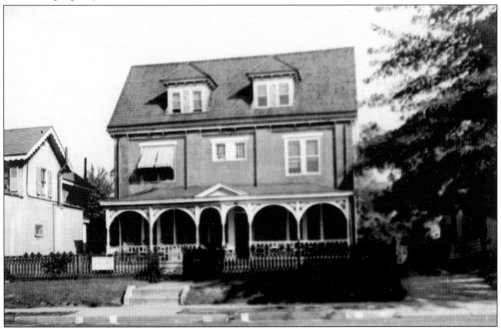

This Broad Street property, located south of Barber Avenue, was once the home of Rev. Daniel Thackara. Built in 1832 as the second house of worship for the Methodists, it was converted into a double dwelling in 1892. This structure, pictured around 1930, was razed in 1957 to make way for the Farmers and Mechanics National Bank, which is known today as Wachovia Bank.

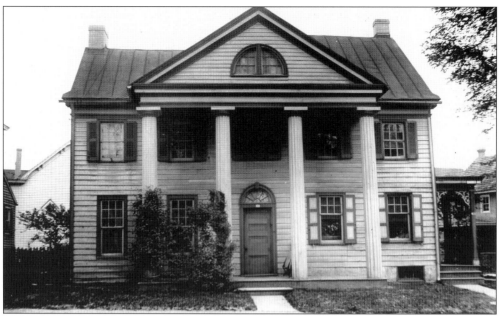

The Pillar or Shute House at the northwest corner of Franklin Street and East Barber Avenue (formerly German Street) still stands today. One of Woodbury's oldest houses, it served as an inn and station where fresh horses were exchanged for the tired ones when stagecoaches operated between intervening towns. It supposedly served as a hospital for wounded Hessians during the Revolutionary War after the battle of Red Bank on October 22, 1777.

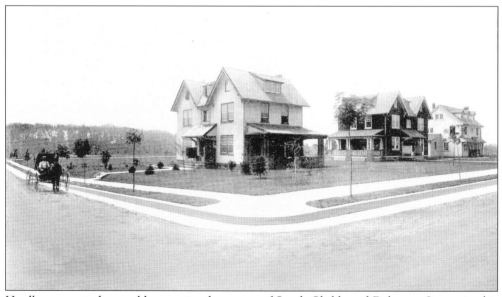

Hardly anyone today would recognize the corner of South Childs and Delaware Streets in this 1913 picture. The Woodbury Realty Company, owners of Bell Tract, constructed 11 residences at the Woodbury Estates housing development. A home could be purchased for a price between $5,700 and $8,400. All the houses were to have modern improvements such as heating, sanitary plumbing, gas and electric fixtures, telephone, and sewer.

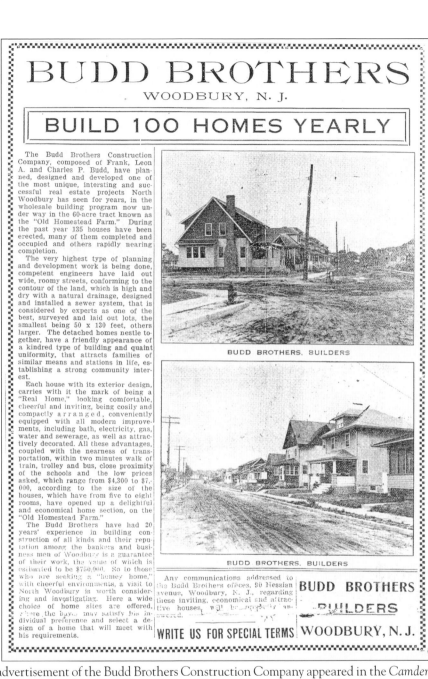
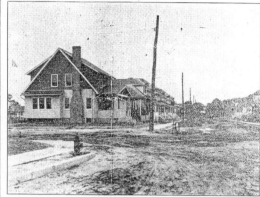

This advertisement of the Budd Brothers Construction Company appeared in the *Camden Argus* on September 20, 1923. The 60-acre tract off Broad Street in North Woodbury was known as the Old Homestead Farm. At this time, Watkins and Crescent Avenues, as well as Tatum Street, were developed. This acreage was subdivided into lots, and the homes that were constructed sold for between $4,300 and $7,000, according to the size of the house and lot. It was during this same time period that Woodbury experienced a building surge on the west side of town. Jacob Heaton and Joseph Potter developed the Schallioll Tract, which bordered Delaware Street on the south, North Girard Street on the east, and Drexel Street on the west. These homes sold for $6,500 and up. Their selling point was that they were located within five minutes from the center of Woodbury.

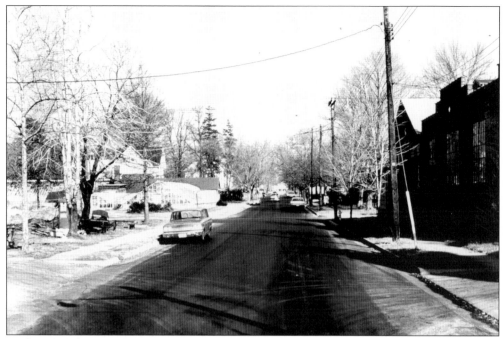

Looking north around 1960 at the intersection of Morris and Logan Streets is Sanderson's Florist and the Cascade Laundry. Today Sanderson's is still a "blooming" business; however, the Cascade Laundry building is vacant.

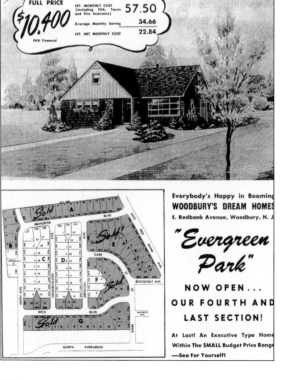

Evergreen Park was advertised as "the 1951 Woodbury New Jersey dream homes." Larry Darms, located at 614 North Broad Street, was the realtor agent for the "most beautiful community in New Jersey." These homes, located on East Red Bank Avenue near the armory, sold for $10,400 and featured two bedrooms, a kitchen with a snack bar, a basement, a spacious living room with a large picture window, a tile bath, and a linen closet.

Seven

RECREATION

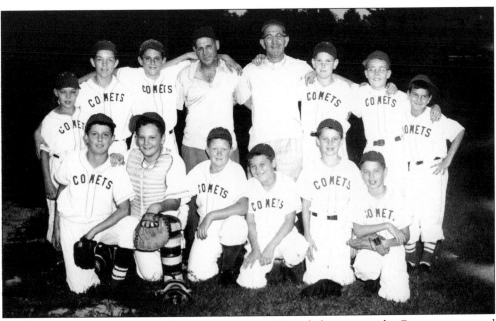

Little League was introduced in Woodbury in May 1951 with four teams: the Comets, sponsored by Cornell and Company; ACE, sponsored by ACE Motors; YMCA, sponsored by the YMCA; and the Rockets, sponsored by Fritchey and Waddell. In pregame ceremonies, Hamilton Lewis, league president, spoke before introducing Mayor Henry Peterson, who then spoke about the city government's endorsement of this supervised youth sports program. He then tossed out the first ball to start the games. In 1952, the league was presented with a loudspeaker system courtesy of the Woodbury Country Club. Plans were also formulated for a field house, which would be constructed for use as a storeroom as well as a concession stand, and an area for announcers and scorekeepers. The 1952 Comets Little League team, pictured from left to right, included (first row) Al Cocciolone, Walt Taylor, Emil Hoelbinger, two unidentified, and John Grosko; (second row) Dan Amey, Walt Trout, Nick Roberts, coach Gilbert (Ikey) Dopson, coach Herb Vogeding, Dave Clemens, Dan Davis, and Marty Finger.

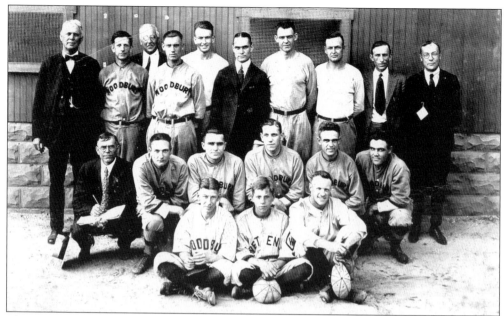

The Woodbury Athletic Club is pictured around 1920 at Page Park on Tatum Street. Pictured from left to right are (first row) Billy Wilson, Howard Dopson, and Frank Fenton; (second row) Charles Umba, Clarence Moyer, Armand "Dutch" Diedrich, Earl Moos, Vic Kugler, and Joe Magee; (third row) Mayor Victor Kugler, Bert Dopson, "Doc" Clark, Joe VanHess, Gene Horan, George Kugler (manager), Neil Deighen, ? Touchstone, Billy Page, and Frank Ackley.

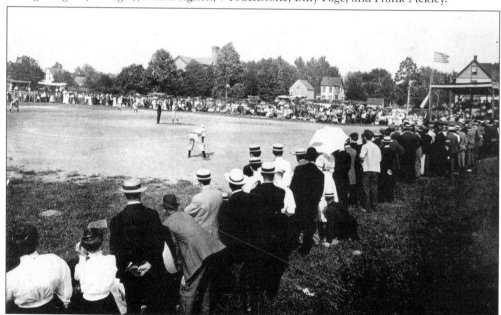

Several hundred people turned out on July 4, 1910, for the much-publicized 10:30 a.m. band concert, followed by a baseball game with the First Ward Athletic Association playing West End at West End Field. The West End boys triumphed by a score of 27-11. A band concert was held at 7:00 p.m. with an hour-long fireworks show starting at 8:00 p.m. for one hour of shooting rockets and a myriad of various colored lights.

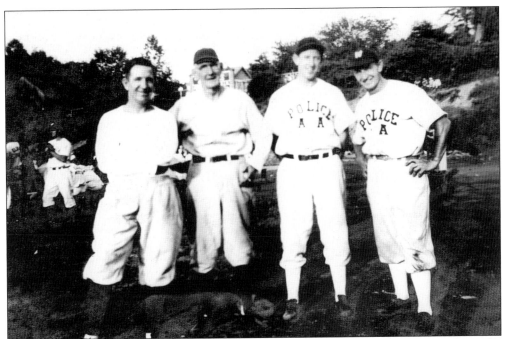

Pictured around 1930 from left to right are Herb, Oscar, Page (Dinger), and John Vogeding, who played for the Police Athletic League Association. The brothers also played numerous other Woodbury sports.

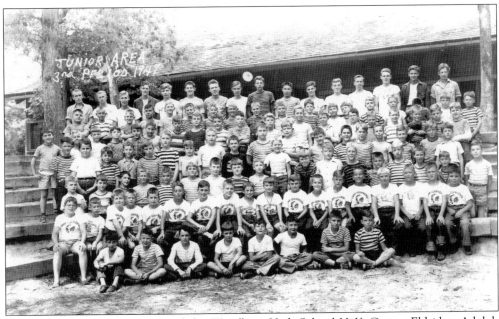

In 1912, the following four started the Woodbury High School Hi-Y: George Eldridge, Adolph Wilsey, Floyd Crispin, and Carrol Haines. The Hi-Y was located in the Green Block building. In 1927, the YMCA relocated to 131 North Broad Street and was open to both boys and girls of high school age. By 1985, they were located on East Red Bank Avenue. Camp Ockanickon in Medford hosted this 1947 YMCA group.

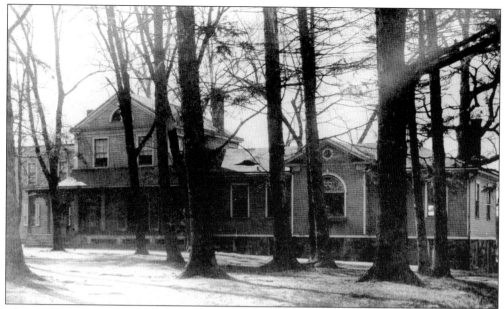

The Woodbury Country Club, pictured around 1902, was incorporated in August 1897 and rapidly grew to 200 members. Dues for the first year were $10 for men and $2.50 for women. The club was established as an all-sports facility, but golf quickly became the focal point. In 1946, a fire destroyed the main section of the building and was quickly rebuilt by Pres. Ralph Cornell at his own expense.

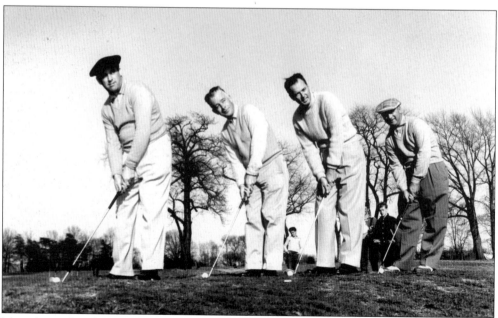

Many have played a round of golf at the Woodbury Country Club. Pictured in 1954, from left to right, are unidentified, Hugh Mehorter, unidentified, and Ralph Cornell. The 50-acre golf course, which borders Cooper Street, Evergreen, and East Barber Avenues, is ranked in the top 200 in the country. The course is nine holes, however, due to limited space, there are two tees on most holes.

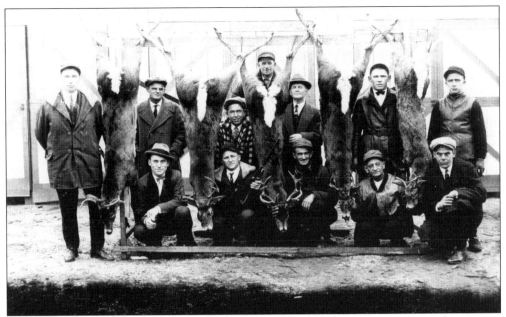

First Ward Antler Club members of Woodbury stand with their trophies from their day's outing. Pictured in 1925 from left to right are (first row) William Robinson, Charles Bengel, Oscar Shoemaker, Joseph Dopson, and William Duffy; (second row) Charles Vennell, Norman Youngcourt, Henry Feltman, Herbert Dopson, Jess Henderson, Cliff Anderson, and Arthur Sheppard.

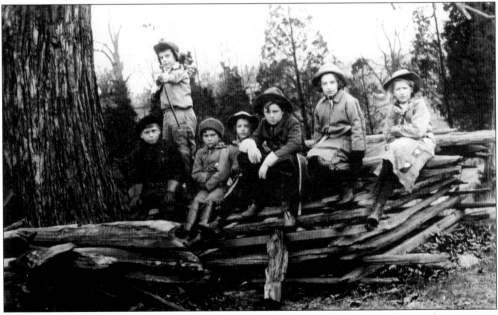

These children enjoy an afternoon of play in the pristine wooded area at the northeast corner of Briar Hill Lane and North Davis Street in 1914. Much of Woodbury's surroundings were still undeveloped and allowed city residents a place to unwind. Pictured from left to right are Charles Thomas, Byron Coy, Harry White, Edie Burrows (Crawford), Gilbert Shivers, Charlotte Burrows, and Virginia McCarthy.

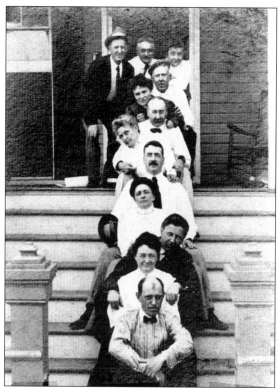

Businessmen from Philadelphia began settling in Woodbury around 1880 after G. G. Green developed Woodbury's East Side. They became know as the "East Side Social Set." Pictured from bottom to top are Mr. and Mrs. George Grove, Mr. and Mrs. William Bonsal, Mr. and Mrs. Edward Green, Judge and Mrs. Lewis Starr, and Mr. and Mrs. Josiah Cloud. From left to right (top) are Dr. Duncan Campbell and Al Harris.

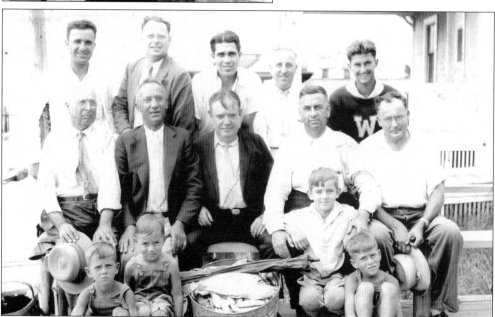

After an extremely rewarding c. 1930 fishing trip, these Woodbury personalities posed for a picture. From left to right are (first row) unidentified, Bob Wilson, Harry F. Wilson, and J. Frank (Bucky) Wilson; (second row) William Snelbaker, Harry Polsky, Emmet Welch, J. Frank Wilson, and unidentified; (third row) Joe Polsky, Wilson Snelbaker, Oscar Davis, unidentified, and Tom Brennan.

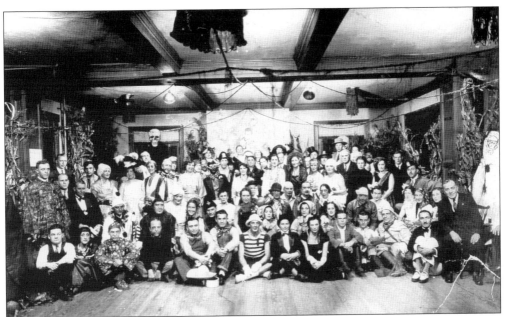

Eureka-Triangle Club members are pictured around 1932 at their Halloween party in the Green Building. The Eureka Club formed in 1914 with 25 members, and the Triangle Club formed in 1915 also with 25 members. With the outbreak of World War I, membership depleted due to the clubs' members going off to fight on foreign soil. In 1917, the clubs merged, and the Eureka-Triangle Club was formed. The organization disbanded in 1934.

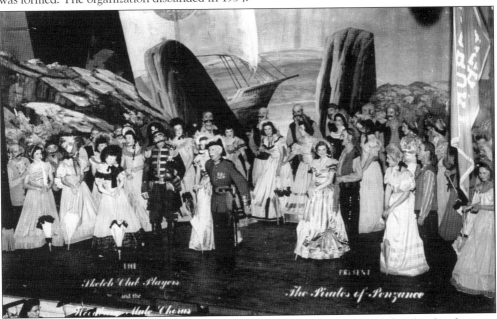

Woodbury Sketch Club performed *The Pirates of Penzance* at Woodbury High School auditorium in November 1948. The club originated in 1933 when a group of culture-minded citizens of Woodbury decided that the community needed an art group. After renting two rooms in the Green Building at West Centre Street for several years, they needed a place to call home and purchased the old West End School building in 1952.

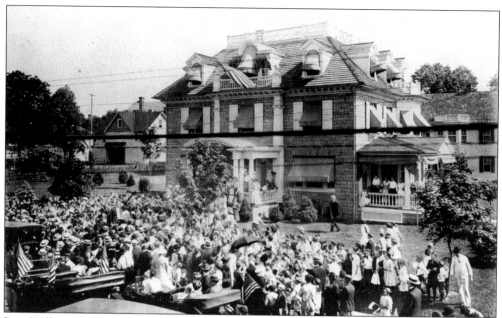

Pres. William Howard Taft arrived on May 28, 1912, via his special train at the Woodbury Station during a campaign tour through Gloucester County. He was quickly conveyed by automobile to the home of school superintendent Daniel T. Steelman on the northeast corner of Cooper and Euclid Streets, where over 1,000 schoolchildren were assembled. After speaking a few words to the children, he proceeded to the courthouse.

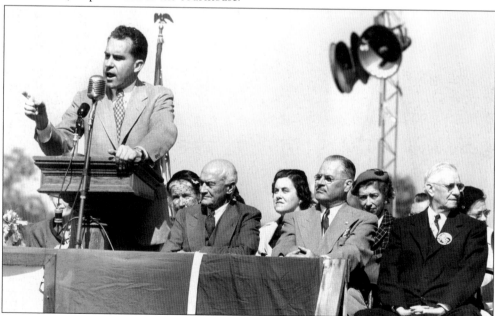

During his one-day tour through the state, Republican vice presidential candidate Richard M. Nixon spoke before an enthusiastic crowd of over 3,000 at Woodbury High School's stadium on October 4, 1952. Senator Nixon encouraged voters that "a vote for Eisenhower is a vote for the best interests of America." From left to right are Nixon, Sen. H. Alexander Smith, Sen. Robert C. Hendrickson, and Congressman Charles Wolverton.

The Republican headquarters of Gloucester County was housed in the Gloucester County Democrat Building. This building formerly housed Tip-Top Men's Shop at 22 South Broad Street. In 1969, the building was the Republican headquarters for William T. Cahill from Haddonfield, who was running for governor. Cahill succeeded and was governor of New Jersey from 1970 to 1974.

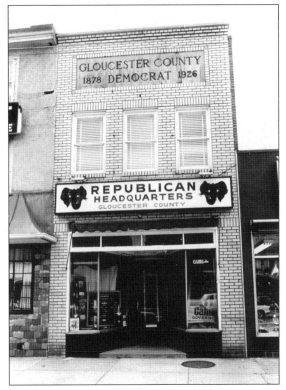

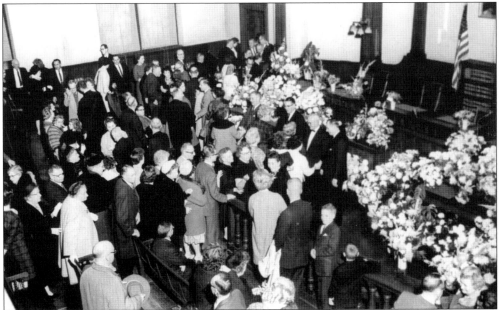

In 1963, the Gloucester County Courthouse on North Broad Street was the scene of swearing-in ceremonies for the sheriff, surrogate, deputy sheriff, and county clerk of Gloucester County. Pictured from left to right facing the crowd in the ceremonial courtroom are John E. Hunt, William C. Strang, Thomas Lyons, and Joseph Hoffman Sr. The November 1962 election determined Sunday sales would now be permitted in the state.

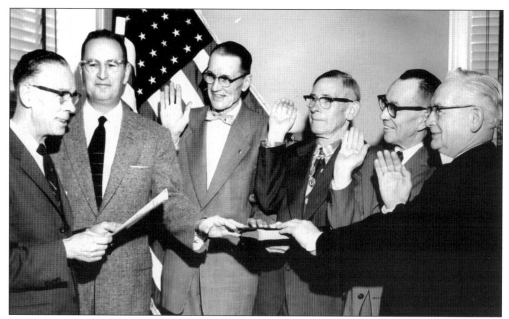

New Jersey celebrated its tercentenary throughout the state in 1964. A Woodbury committee was formed in 1961 with the following members, from left to right: Mayor Walter Trout, chairman Dr. Warren McClain, Frank Hogarth, Russell Archut, J. Sennett Holston, and Ernest Zimmerman. Local festivities included a commemorative booklet, open house tours of houses and gardens, special Fourth of July festivities, and a Woodbury Day at the New York World's Fair.

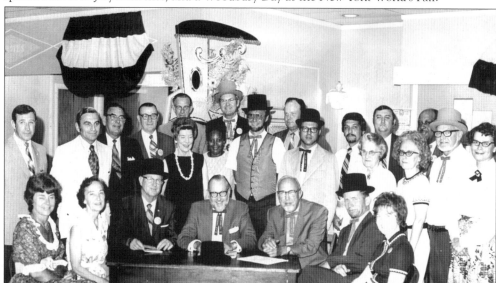

Woodbury's Centennial Incorporation Committee members in 1971, from left to right included (first row) Terry Johnson, Gertrude Brumund, Robert Brumund, Robert Boakes, Alfred Hill, Amos Peaslee, and Shirley Becker (Bierbrunner); (second row) John Turnock, Frederick Thompson, William Strang, Michael McGuinness, William Suback, Laurie Smedley, Mrs. Waples Sr., Perry Johnson, Herbert Budd Jr., Walter Fish, Roy Duffield, Michael Angelastro, Richard Caton, Margaret Beck, Dorothy Ballinger, Calvin Waples Sr., William Lovegrove, and Edith Hoelle.

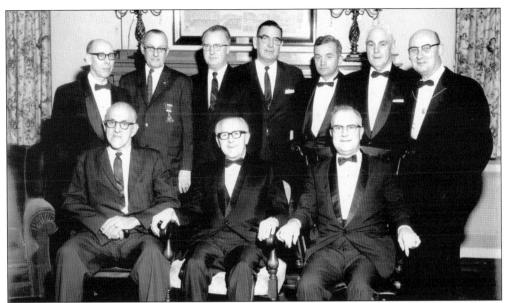

Woodbury's Florence Lodge, No. 87, F. and A. M. was formed in January 1868. Meetings were held in the Odd Fellows' Hall on Delaware Street until the Masonic temple on North Broad Street was dedicated in 1926. The 100th anniversary committee in 1968, from left to right, included (first row) Edmund Haines, Morgan Morris, and Charles Floyd; (second row) William Philipp, William Wakemen, Ernest Polk, William Strang, Samuel Fuss, Stokley Ramsey, and John Manning.

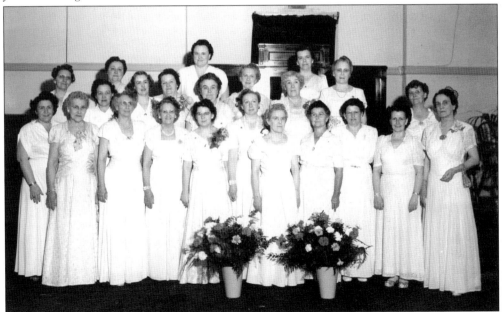

The Order of the Eastern Star No. 109 was formed in Woodbury in 1919 with Laura Wilson and Preston Rice as first matron and patron. It was created to be a female branch of Freemasonry with members 18 years or older and properly related to a master Mason in good standing. This picture was taken in April 1948 at the installation of officers with Norman and Jane Brous as patron and matron.

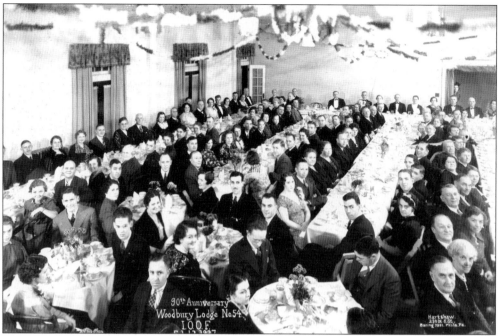

The Woodbury Lodge No. 54 Independent Order of Odd Fellows' 90th anniversary dinner was held on February 12, 1937, at the Pitman Golf Club. Ernest Redfield, past grand master and well-known historian, gave a historical discourse on the growth of the lodge, which was organized on February 4, 1847. Weekly meetings began in a building behind Friendship Fire House and later convened in the Moose hall on Cooper Street.

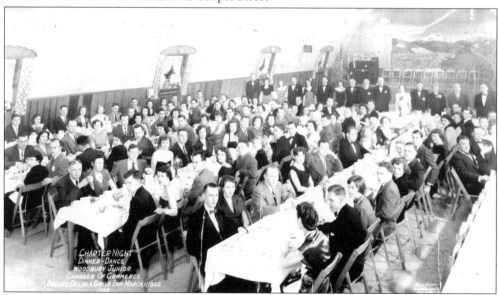

The Woodbury Junior Chamber of Commerce (Jaycees) charter night dinner was held on March 11, 1950, at Oscar's Delsea Drive Inn in Clayton. The guest speaker was U.S. senator Robert Hendrickson. Organized in 1949 by Bob Boakes, the organization held meetings in private homes and later in the American Legion Hall. The Jaycees sponsored the Woodbury Fall Parade, Miss Gloucester County Pageant, Post Prom Party, and the annual Fourth of July fireworks.

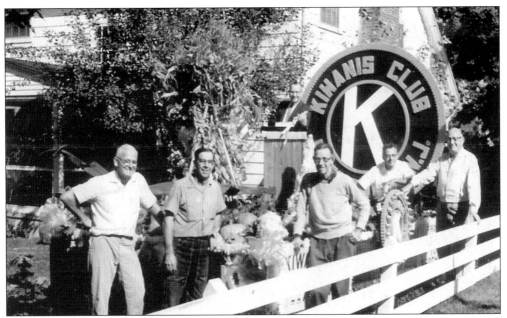

Members of the Woodbury Kiwanis Club posed with their award-winning float in Howard Ballinger's backyard on Delaware Street. They had constructed the floats for the Woodbury Fall Parade in 1966. Pictured from left to right are Ballinger, Charles Osman, Bill Suback, Joe Johnson, Oscar Books, and Bob Boakes at the podium. The club, formed in 1923 with 50 members, is still active today in the community.

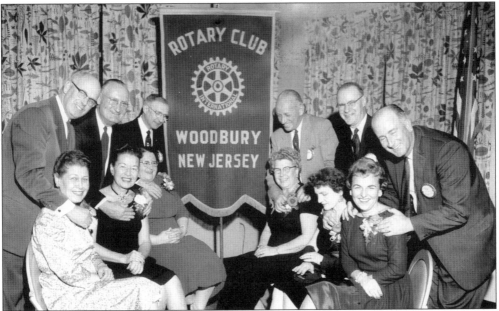

Woodbury Lunch Rotary, a member of Rotary International, was chartered with 25 members in 1921. They met in the Homestead Restaurant on South Broad Street until moving to the Woodbury Country Club. Pictured in 1959 from left to right are (front row) Mrs. Sax, Ann Lee, Leona Foster, Jane Brous, Rose MacNeil, and Dorothy Eastlack; (second row) Robert Sax, Robert Lee, district governor Benjamin Foster, Norman Brous, Elwell MacNeil, and Clayton Eastlack.

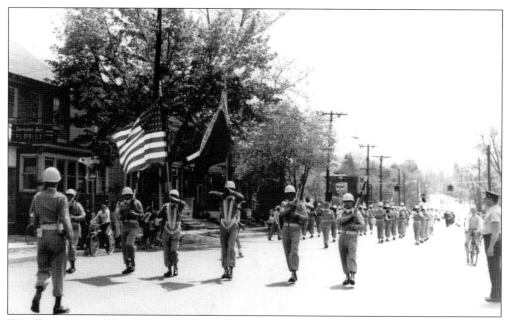

Woodbury's Bonsal Blues march up North Broad Street in 1960 with band director Robert Taylor. The band was named for William Stokes Bonsal, a Woodbury resident killed in World War I. They took the name Blues in memory of the Jersey Blues of the Revolutionary War. Brothers Bob and Bert Boakes are credited with starting the military band in 1948 with Woodbury alumni who had been in World War II.

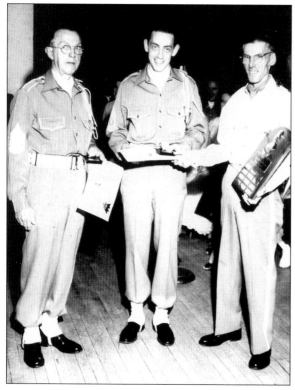

On April 12, 1958, the John Philip Sousa award was presented to Bonsal Blues band members (from left to right) Roy Jackson (band librarian) and Lindley Carpenter (president) by director Robert Taylor. This was the first time a non-school band was honored with this award. The Bonsal Blues continues to hold concerts and participate in local parades today.

On Memorial Day, May 30, 1963, Mayor Walter Trout, atop the steps of the courthouse, stressed that the American public should get back to "the old beliefs in such things as ideals, pride, patriotism, devotion and unity of purpose." The Bonsal Blues Band, followed by the parade marshal Edward Baker, led the parade. Former U.S. senator Robert Hendrickson and councilman Michael McGuinness spoke at the Presbyterian and Green Cemeteries, respectively.

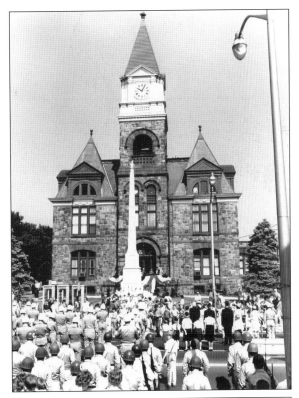

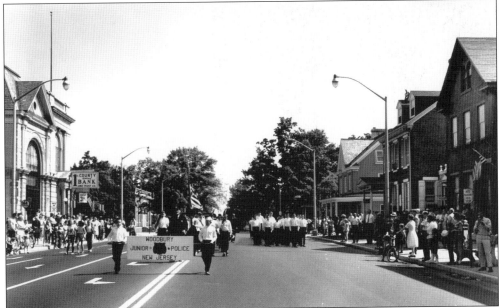

The Woodbury Junior Police Reserve was featured for the first time in the 1963 Memorial Day Parade. The reserve, 120 strong in the line of march down Broad Street, included its own drum and bugle corps of 35 members. The Veterans of Foreign Wars Post No. 2117, American Legion Post, Jewish War Veterans Post No. 604, Jewish War Veterans of World War I No. 1740, and the National Guard were also represented.

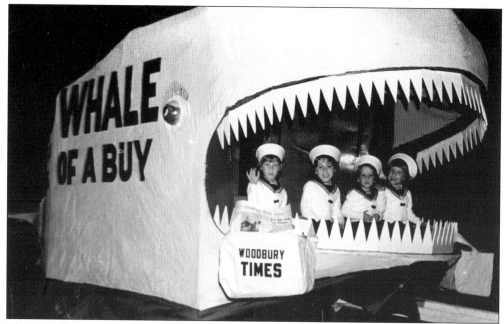

The Woodbury Fall Parade held in October was always a crowd pleaser with numerous high school bands, floats, Boy and Girl Scout troops, and fire engines. The *Gloucester County Times* float entry in this 1966 photograph suggests that the paper was a "whale of a buy." Pictured from left to right are Carol Wilson, Joanne Wilson, Sue Lightcap, and Kim Wilson.

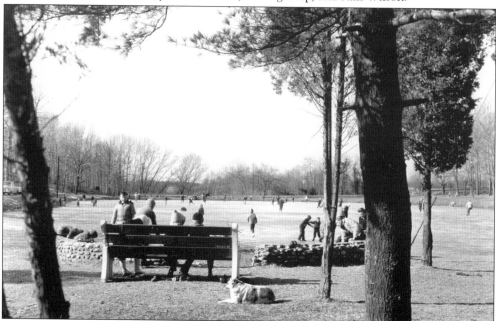

Children of all ages enjoy ice-skating at Bell Lake on January 14, 1962. The lake, bounded by South Girard Street and Myrtle Avenue, was developed by Samuel Bell after he purchased a farm on the west side of Woodbury about 1902 and erected six houses. Bell later moved to Washington Township and established Bell's Lake. His grandfather, Isaiah, was the founder of General Mills Inc. of Minneapolis.